THE BIG BOOK O' BEER

Library of Congress Cataloging in Publication Number: 2003113712

ISBN: 1-931686-49-1

Printed in Singapore

Typeset in Rockwell, Rotis, Serpentine

Designed by Bryn Ashburn
Illustrations on pages 43–77, 98, 101, 113, 115, 128, 131, 133, 134–135 by Matt Madden
Illustrations on pages 40–41, 138–139, 156, 161 by Bryn Ashburn and Karen Onorato
Photography on the cover, pages 3, 25, 29–31, 44, 95–96, 102-105, 108, 122–125, 135, 176,
178 by William Drake
Photography on pages 8, 26, 78, 80, 95–96, 102, 105, 116, 118–121, 125, 129, 130, 132,
137, 142, 162, 171–175, 190 by Bryn Ashburn

Distributed in North America by Chronicle Books
85 Second Street
San Francisco, CA 94105

10 9 8 7 6 5 4 3 2 1

Quirk Books
215 Church Street
Philadelphia, PA 19106
www.quirkbooks.com

HISTORY · FAMOUS BARS · DRINKING GAMES

The
BIG BOOK O'
BEER

by DUANE SWIERCZYNSKI

Everything You Ever Wanted
to Know About the Greatest
Beverage on Earth

BEER CAN CRAFTS · TOASTS · VINTAGE CANS

QUIRK BOOKS
PHILADELPHIA

CONTENTS

THIS BOOK IS FOR SARAH EVELYN.
I'M LOOKING FORWARD TO THE DAY
WHEN SHE'LL SHARE HER FIRST BEER
WITH HER DAD.

INTRODUCTION

ONE HUNDRED BOTTLES OF BEER ON MY WALL

Great literature demands great sacrifices.

George Orwell spent months living as a dirty, penniless hobo to gather material for his ground-breaking *Down and Out in Paris and London*. In the early 1960s, William Howell Masters and Virginia Eshelman Johnson spent the better part of the decade observing the sexual practices of some 700 men and women to produce a startlingly honest survey of human sexuality, *Human Sexual Response*. To reconstruct the 1988 presidential election in his 1992 political masterpiece *What It Takes*, Richard Ben Cramer spent three years transcribing thousands of hours of interviews with the candidates.

So when I was granted the opportunity to write a book-length paean to the world's greatest beverage—beer—I made a bold decision.

I would drink 100 different bottles of beer.

This was not as easy as it sounds. Sacrifices were made; laws were broken. In my home state of Pennsylvania, for instance, you can only purchase beer by the case or six-pack. To purchase individual bottles of different beers, I had to journey all the way out to New Jersey. Bringing the beers back to Pennsylvania was punishable by huge fines and even prison terms, but I took the risk. (I also hid the bottles beneath my son's baby stroller, so the cops wouldn't see them.)

Drinking the beer wasn't easy, either. While most of the brews I sampled were delicious and soul-nourishing—the equivalent of pressing my taste buds to the beaches of heaven—some were a little more challenging. More than a few imported beers must have spent a couple of extra months on the boat, because upon opening them, I caught the whiff of stale air reminiscent of a freshly opened Romanian tomb. Others smelled like feet. And my American sensibilities weren't quite ready for one variety of German *rauchbier* (translation: smoke beer) that tasted like somebody left a strip of bacon in a glass of porter overnight.

But it was worth the trouble. My goal was to write an unabashed, unashamed, unbridled love letter to beer, the greatest beverage on earth. It was to be a guided tour through the world of beer, from pilsner to porter, from suds to sediment, from highbrow to Löwenbräu. I could only do that, I reasoned, by dipping my cup repeatedly into the vast barrel of world beer, and exploring the outer limits of malted grains, hops, and yeast.

So what did I learn after drinking more than 100 different bottles of beer?

To be honest, I'm not entirely sure—the revelations elude me, like Coleridge struggling to make sense of his feverish vision of Xanadu. I might have to get back to you on that after my next hundred bottles.

Such are the sacrifices of literature.

THE HISTORY OF BEER

"Without question, the greatest invention in the history of mankind

is beer. Oh, I grant you that the wheel was also a fine invention, but

the wheel does not go nearly as well with pizza."—*Dave Barry*

Get up and go to your fridge. Take out a can of Budweiser. See that "Born On" date? It's a lie. Your can of beer wasn't born back on March 30. It wasn't even born during this century. Beer first appeared on this planet thousands and thousands of years ago, after which the earth would never be the same. Forget everything you learned in high school history. Modern civilization is totally and completely a result of beer. It transformed early man from a scrappy group of hunter/gatherers into a tight-knit posse of hunter/beer drinkers. Here's how it happened.

GREAT MOMENTS IN BEER HISTORY: ANTIQUITY

Who brewed the first beer in history? Nobody knows for sure. Some think beer might have been invented by accident, after a sudden thunderstorm drenched a stockpile of barley, berries, grapes, or honey kept by ancient hunter/gatherers in Sumer (now Iraq). Once the fruit or grains were soaked, they began to ferment, thanks to natural airborne yeasts. Then some brave soul gathered up a cup of the frothy result, and primitive beer was born. And later, possibly, hurled.

Beer's effects were immediately noticeable. There's even an ancient Sumerian proverb that says, "No children without sex—no drunkenness without beer." People started to settle down to farm, mostly to harvest the grains needed to make beer and maybe the occasional loaf of bread. But there's no denying that between the dawn of man and the first glimmer of the Renaissance, there was a whole lot of beer drinking going on. Here are some ancient taproom highlights.

50000 TO 20000 B.C.

Noah packs beer on the Ark, along with his wife, kids, and two of every animal. (This is not specifically shown in the painting below, but recorded in Assyrian tablets dating back to 2000 B.C.) Hopefully, God instructed him to bring more than two sixes, considering the deluge was to last 40 days and 40 nights.

2600 B.C. (CIRCA)

The ancient Sumerians brew beer, store it in pottery, and sip it through straws. Yes, straws. Ancient beer was often full of unpleasant-tasting grain hulls left behind after the crude brewing process. In the cylinder seal shown here, you can glimpse a man and a woman sharing a beer in the top left corner. And they have enough straws left over for three friends!

2500 B.C. (CIRCA)

The Egyptians brew beer—they called it *heqet* or *hekt*—of the fruity variety, and it becomes the beverage of choice for adults and children alike. The wooden carving shown here depicts an Egyptian woman filtering barley bread to make beer.

1800 B.C. (CIRCA)

The Babylonians—the guys who took over Mesopotamia after the Sumerians—whip out the soft clay tablets and mark down recipes for some 20 varieties of beer. According to a recent archeological dig in northern Syria, here's what the Babylonians had on tap: "Dark Beer," "Beer of Two Parts," "Pale Beer," "Red Beer," "Beer from Down Below," "Beer with a Head," and (I kid you not) "Beer Without a Head."

1795 TO 1750 B.C.

Babylonian ruler Hammurabi introduces the first written laws—some of which apply to beer. In fact, the beer laws appear higher than any of those dumb laws about family responsibility.

1350 B.C.

A set of Egyptian hieroglyphics from the reign of Ramses II (at right) reveals the earliest known form of drinking advice: "Make not thyself helpless in drinking in the beer shop / For will not the word of thy report repeated slip out from thy mouth without thy knowing that thou hast uttered them."

1250 B.C.

Jews wandering in the desert receive manna from heaven. Nineteenth-century anthropologist James Death theorized that manna was actually a kind of beer-based porridge called *wusa*. If it's true, that explains why the Jews took so long to find their way. The ancient beer jugs shown at left are of the same era and feature built-in strainers.

1000 B.C. (CIRCA)
ONE NOT-SO-GREAT MOMENT

The Egyptians come up with nonalcoholic beer. No wonder the Jews left.

400 B.C. (CIRCA)

The Greek playwright Sophocles writes: "I recommend bread, meat, vegetables, and beer." For this, I recommend Sophocles's plays.

49 B.C.

Julius Caesar (at left) hosts a massive beer bash for his troops after they cross the Rubicon, an event that kicks off the Roman Civil War. Even though most snobby Romans were wine drinkers, the Romans called beer *cerevisia* after Ceres, the Roman goddess of agriculture.

A.D. 500

Saint Bridget (at left) allegedly turns water into beer, according to the *Vita Sanctae Brigidae* (a.k.a. *The Life of Saint Bridget*). "For when the lepers she nursed implored her for beer and there was none to be had, she changed the water which was ready for a bath into an excellent brew, by the sheer strength of her blessing."

A.D. 630 (CIRCA)

In Belgium, Saint Arnold of Metz dips his crucifix into a vat of beer, then tells local villagers, "Don't drink the water, drink beer." Legend claims that those who sipped from the blessed vat were cured of a plague that had been going around.

A.D. 700 TO 900

The Vikings run the most hardcore beer party the world has ever seen, according to Alan D. Eames's book, *The Secret Life of Beer: Legends, Lore, and Little-Known Facts*. These Norse ale-heads raped and pillaged pretty much every country they'd heard of—England, Ireland, France, Germany, Italy—all the while drunk on casks of beer.

FUN VIKING FACTS:

- They enjoyed lopping off their enemies' heads, ripping away the flesh, boiling the skull, and using it as a beer mug. If you wanted to bond with a fellow Viking forever, you had to drip some of your own blood into his skull mug, and vice versa.
- The Vikings loved to trick their enemies into getting really wasted in an ale house, only to torch the house later, roasting everyone inside.
- According to Viking law, whatever you said while drunk was legally binding. Did you boast that you could kick Utgard's arse with one hand tied behind your back? Better start practicing those left hooks.

A.D. 800

European monasteries—especially in Holland and Belgium—get into the beer business, and soon monks become the world's brewing experts. Locals and travelers stop by to purchase ale, which in turn funds the monasteries. Beer and religion have always been closely intertwined; medieval brewers didn't know how yeast worked—or that it even existed—but they knew the effects were miraculous, so they called the mysterious agent "God Is Good." Damn good.

A.D. 1200

Throughout Europe, it becomes customary to baptize children with beer.

Really, Really Old Beer

~ what beer tasted like thousands of years ago? Besides warm? In 1989, mpany in San Francisco decided to celebrate the 10-year anniversary of its oking up something much, much older: 5,000-year-old Sumerian beer. T tz—a University of Pennsylvania archeologist who specializes in ancient nd with the recipe, and used the "Hymn to Ninkasi", a poem praising th orewing, as their guide. The result, called "Essay, August 1989," was a hop eer that had the distinct flavor of honey and dates. If you were around ~ of 1989, you could have tried it, but since "Essay, August 1989" lacked bility to last very long.

rs later, Katz and his Penn colleague, Pat McGovern, analyzed the remains 2,700-year-old tomb of King Midas (shown above) in central Turkey, and his grieving subjects most likely got blasted on a kind of barley bee n Caglione at the Dogfish Head Brewery in Rehoboth Beach, Delaware, t version of this King Midas beer. The result was dubbed "Midas Touch," an honey, muscat grapes, barley, and saffron. (You don't have to hold a degr ogy to try some, either. Just visit www.dogfish.com, and click on "Our Be

GREAT MOMENTS IN BEER HISTORY: ENLIGHTENMENT

Folks in the Middle Ages had the right idea about beer. In England, it was common practice to have "elevenses," a beer break at 11 A.M. to "nourish the body and spirit." (Try to have elevenses today, and you can expect to be in the human resources office by twosies.) After a long day of trading, the English would retire to the local beer hall and enjoy a nice large pot of ale with their dinners—and possibly more ale when they returned home, where their spouses and children would be sipping beer, too.

In the Middle Ages, beer was worshipped and heavily consumed for a good reason—nobody wanted to drink the water. Fluoride? Please. Towns and municipalities could barely filter the raw sewage out of their drinking supplies. Beer was the beverage of choice for men, women, and children because the brewing process was guaranteed to strain out most of the nastiness. Even Queen Elizabeth I made a point of starting every morning with a cup of strong ale. Over the next 400 years, beer continued to inspire mankind and influence history—including the founding of one obscure country called the United States of America.

1516

The *Reinheitsgebot*—that's the famous "German Purity Law"—is introduced. The law states that you can only use four ingredients in beer: malted barley, malted wheat, hops, and water. (These guys were still dependent on wild airborne yeasts to achieve fermentation.) Historians call this one of the first consumer-protection laws; the document (at right) protected German beer lovers from no-goodnik brewers who tried to use cheap sugar in their lousy beers. The punishment? "Whosoever knowingly disregards or transgresses upon this ordinance, shall be punished by the Court authorities confiscating such barrels of beer, without fail."

1600s

Midwives create "Groaning Ale," a special beer meant to ease the pain of childbirth. This ultrapowerful beer would be fermented in casks for seven or eight months, then tapped when the contractions began. (Sounds better than an epidural, doesn't it?) Some midwives would even bathe the newborn in beer, since it was likely to be cleaner than water available at the time.

1614

The first nonnative American is born on the southern tip of New Amsterdam—later to become lower Manhattan. His name is Jean Vigne, and he is born inside the first known American brewhouse, Block and Christiansen's, which opened two years earlier. Even better, little Jean would grow up to become a brewer and America's first natural-born beer maker.

1620

Puritans on the Mayflower decide to hit the coast around Plymouth not because it looked attractive—full of amber waves of grain and all that—but because the ship was running out of beer. The seamen ditched their passengers so the crew would have enough brew to make it back to England. (According to the ship's log, the passengers "were hasted ashore and made to drink water that the seamen might have the more beer.") The Puritans immediately began construction on their own brewhouse.

1754

George Washington (at left) cobbles together his own beer recipe and records it in his notebook.

George Washington's "Small Beer" Recipe

George Washington may have grown up among cherry trees, but his adult interests were chiefly hops and barley. He enjoyed the art of home brewing, and while serving with the British troops during the French and Indian War, he came up with his own recipe for "small beer." ("Small beer" is an old term for a light, less-filling beer; in other words, the beer to drink when you're having more than three.) Here is Washington's recipe, in his own words:

"Take a large Siffer full of Bran Hops to your taste—Boil these 3 hours [then] strain out 30 Gallns into a cooler put in 3 Gallns molasses while the beer is scalding hot or rather draw the molasses into the cooler & strain the beer on it while boiling hot. Let this stand till it is little more than Blood warm then put in a quart of yeast if the weather is very cold cover it over with a blanket & let it work in the Cooler 24 hours then put it into the Cask—leave it the Bung open till it is almost done Working—Bottle it that day [the next] Week [after] it was brewed."

1774

In August, amateur British scientist Joseph Priestley visits a brewery down the street from his house. While there, he ponders the bubbles rising from a vat of beer—an observation that leads to his discovery of oxygen.

1775

Revolutionary War soldiers are given rations of a quart of beer per day. This is one of the first acts of the brand-spanking-new Continental Congress.

1777

On September 13, Frederick the Great, King of Prussia, announces: "My people must drink beer. His majesty was brought up on beer and so were his ancestors and his officers and soldiers. Many battles have been fought and won by soldiers nourished on beer, and the King does not believe that coffee-drinking soldiers can be depended on to endure hardships or to beat the enemies." Long live the king!

1809

U.S. President James Madison (at right) tries to establish a National Brewery and appoint a "Secretary of Beer" to his cabinet. His efforts fail, but just think how incredibly cool this would have been.

1810

Prince Ludwig of Bavaria gets hitched to Princess Theresa. So what, you ask? Well, their wedding reception turned into a 16-day beer party, one that was repeated the following year. Soon it became known as "Oktoberfest," giving young blonde girls in billowy blouses a reason to lug around oversized beer steins.

1814

Twenty people in London, England, drown after 4,000 casks of beer accidentally burst, unleashing a 25-foot-high (7.6-m) tidal wave of ale in a residential part of the city (near Tottenham Court Road). Rescue efforts are hampered by thirsty beer lovers who swarm to the scene, scooping up as much free beer as they can. (I gave plenty of serious thought to making this a "not-so-great moment," but let's be honest: there are far, far worse ways to go.)

1836

ONE NOT-SO-GREAT MOMENT

The idea of beer abstinence, or "teetotalism," is first introduced by the United States Temperance Union. Illustrations like the one shown here begin to appear like dark clouds across the horizon.

1842

The first golden lager is created in Pilsen, Bohemia. It takes the name of the town, and is henceforth known as "pilsner." Over 90 percent of the beer produced worldwide today is pilsner.

1876

Scientific genius Louis Pasteur figures out how to make beer last longer. Today, most people associate Pasteur with milk, unaware that he originally came up with "pasteurization" while trying to keep beer from spoiling. In his landmark 1876 paper, "Études sur la Bière" (translation: "Studies on Beer"), Pasteur wrote that "flash heating" beer killed bacteria that caused it to spoil within days of being bottled.

1883

On May 24, Piels Brewery opens in East New York, Brooklyn. (The Brooklyn Bridge opens for business the same day, which makes it easier for people from Manhattan to receive beer from Piels. Coincidence?)

1890s

Back in the Old West, womenfolk weren't welcome in saloons. But Martha Jane Cannary Burk (at right)—who would later be known as "Calamity Jane"—played by her own rules. After all, she had lived a rough-and-tumble life full of gunslinging, mail running, exotic dancing, and prostitution. She even claimed to have been one of General Custer's scouts back in 1870. Barkeeps couldn't refuse the little lady a beer when she stormed into saloons and shouted, "I'm Calamity Jane, and the drinks are on me!"

1909

Before heading off for an African safari, former U.S. President Teddy Roosevelt (at right) packs his socks, underwear, and more than 500 gallons (1891 l) of beer.

1910

In December, The German Brewing Company in Cumberland, Maryland, tries to convince the general public that beer is healthier than water. From the advertisement: "Dr. F. E. Harrington, City Health Officer, who is fighting disease, says after making several analyses, that much of the city water is not fit to drink! Why not avoid all risk and USE GERMAN BEER! It is pleasing to the taste and good for your system. Phone us and have a case sent home. You'll like it."

TREE OF INTEMPERANCE

BY A. D. FILLMORE.

This 1855 illustration by A. D. Fillmore shows the benefits of temperance and the evils of drink. The banner that reads "Hurrah! for the Maine law" refers to the Maine Liquor Law of 1851, which made Maine the first "dry" state (nearly 70 years before national prohibition went into effect).

NOT-SO-GREAT MOMENTS IN BEER HISTORY: PROHIBITION

Prohibition crept onto the shores of the United States right before the great and terrible First World War. One can almost—*almost*, I say—understand why you might want to wrap chains around Demon Rum or its five devious sisters (whiskey, tequila, vodka, brandy, and gin). But beer? Wholesome, invigorating, fortifying beer? Cradle of civilization? Tamer of kings? Nectar of the gods? Yet, the unthinkable happened. Beer was lumped in with the rest of booze, and for 13 awful years, not one legal drop of precious amber fluid could be found between San Francisco and New York City. Serious beer fans moved to Europe for the duration, bucked the law and found speakeasies, or brewed their own at home.

How the hell did this happen? During the 1800s, there were various attempts at a national prohibition, and some states even chose to go dry for a while. But it wasn't until the eve of World War I that momentum grew enough for Prohibition to become scary reality. Reform was in the air, and some do-gooders thought that by getting rid of booze and saloons, fathers would report home to take care of their families, crime would plummet, and the United States would be a happier, safer country. Boy, were they wrong.

1915

There are about 1,400 operating breweries in the United States. A temperance group called the Anti-Saloon League lobbies for a constitutional amendment that prohibits liquor, but the plan is shot down when it fails to receive a two-thirds majority vote (197 were for it, 190 against). Beer drinkers breathe a sign of relief, but the worst is yet to come.

1919

Nuts. In January, Congress ratifies the 18th Amendment, prohibiting the transportation, manufacture, import, or sale of "intoxicating liquors." In October, the Volstead Act—named for its architect, Rep. Andrew J. Volstead, of Minnesota—is passed, which defines "intoxicating liquors" as anything that's more than 0.5 percent alcohol. Thousands of beers are destroyed. (The photo at right depicts just one of these mindless slaughters.)

1920

Prohibition officially goes into effect. Gangsters and bootleggers start killing each other in vicious bids for control of the illegal booze market. No one suffers more than beer drinkers (it's far easier to bootleg bottles of cheap gin than to smuggle a barrel of beer into the country). Beer becomes very hard to find. "Once, during Prohibition, I was forced to live on nothing but food and water," quips W. C. Fields.

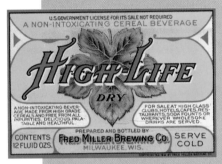

1921

Brewers, suddenly out of customers, produce 300 million gallons (1.14 billion l) of "near beer." Miller brews a no-alcohol version of High-Life. Pabst comes up with something called "Pablo." Schlitz gives the world "Famo." All of these products are Crap-O. In the words of one beer lover who suffered through these times, "A person who called it near beer was a pretty poor judge of distance." Since breweries had no way to predict if Prohibition would ever end, most went out of business. Thousands of workers lost their jobs.

1922

ONE GREAT MOMENT

Representative Andrew Volstead gets volsteaded out of public office in Minnesota and returns to his career as a lawyer.

1925

There are reports that bartenders at speakeasies toss a shot of ethyl alcohol into near beer, just to give it some extra zing. This is a crime against both beer and humanity.

1926

Representative John Philip Hill of Maryland leads the Wet Party, a political group devoted to ending Prohibition. In this publicity still, Hill illustrates his commitment to spreading "wetness" throughout the globe.

1929

The Great Depression kicks in. This is not exactly a great time to be alive and in America.

1930

The American Brewers Association is formed, despite the fact that there's not much worth brewing anymore. But momentum for repeal is growing at fever pitch— with the Depression in full swing, anti-Prohibitionists argue that a repeal would create thousands of much-needed jobs.

1932

At last, a glimmer of hope: The Democratic Party endorses the repeal of Prohibition, as does its presidential candidate, Franklin Delano Roosevelt. FDR wins later that year by a landslide. Go figure.

1933

After exactly 13 years, 10 months, 19 days, 17 hours and 32^1/2 minutes, Prohibition ends nationwide on December 5. Upon ratifying the 21st Amendment (which nixed the 18th Amendment), President Roosevelt says, "I believe that this would be a good time for a beer!"

GREAT MOMENTS IN BEER HISTORY: MODERNITY

Sanity resumed; beer was legal again. And just in time, too—war was about to break out, and Nehru jackets were on the horizon. But it took a while for beer to recover from the blow of Prohibition. After 1933, beer—once a staple of everyone's diet, from children to senior citizens—somehow adopted a rough-and-tumble veneer, and became a beverage enjoyed solely by old men, working Joes, college students, and ladies of ill repute. The stigma of Prohibition killed off dozens of companies. By 1983, there were only 80 breweries left in the United States (down from 1,400 in 1915) and these were run by only 51 different companies.

It was a dire century for the greatest beverage on earth, but thankfully this story has a happy ending. By the 1990s, with the advent of craft beers and microbreweries, beer started to regain the respect it had enjoyed throughout millennia. Today, even Joe Six-Pack has access to beer styles and varieties—fruit beers, barley wine beers, chicory beers—that haven't been available for thousands of years.

1935

The beer can is introduced, and the next 70 years bring startling, crowd-pleasing can innovations. (For more, see "The Evolution of the Beer Can," page 28.)

1942

The U.S. Government's War Production Board encourages beer lovers to buy quarts instead of bottles, all in an effort to conserve the metal used in bottle caps. Some brewers start running ridiculously un-P.C. ad slogans, such as SAVE CAPS TO BEAT THE JAPS.

1942

ONE NOT-SO-GREAT MOMENT

In an effort to ration tin and metal, canned beer is prohibited in the United States. Only soldiers overseas are allowed to drink beer from cans.

1944

Jazz singer Billie Holiday—on her deathbed with cirrhosis of the liver—asks her nurse for a daily glass of beer, only to chide her for her lack of serving skills. "What kind of trained nurse are you, baby, if you can't pour a beer?"

War and Beer

War and beer have walked hand in hand ever since the first Viking went berserk, tossed away his opaque plastic cup, and decided to use his enemy's empty skull as a beer container instead (see page 13). There is a long history of nations supplying their armed forces with mass quantities of beer, and the twentieth century is no exception.

World War I sucked for the U.S. military. Prohibition was on the horizon back at home, and nobody thought that giving beer to hardworking defenders of liberty was a good idea. During World War II, however, the government happily supplied Our Boys with cans of beer (Ballantine's and Fort Litt) painted drab olive, so as not to reflect light and make the soldiers easy targets. In 1943, all brewers were required to allocate 15 percent of their beer supply for military use.

Today, the military beer tradition continues, but for some enlisted men, you have to wait for a special "beer day." Navy tradition has it that sailors who have gone 45 days or more without shore leave are entitled to kick back and enjoy a beer or two. But in early 2003, sailors on the USS *Camden*, deployed in the Persian Gulf, were getting worried: "beer day" was falling on Ash Wednesday, a day when Catholic beer-lovers are supposed to fast, and therefore give up the suds. Fortunately, the ship's chaplain, Ron Nordan, received an e-mail dispensation from higher-ranking chaplains, and Catholic Navy sailors were able to enjoy their beer guilt-free.

1958

The American Medical Association publishes a study by Noah D. Fabrican, a Chicago otolaryngologist, who says beer might be helpful in fighting the common cold.

1967

In May, the Meister Brau Brewing Company in Chicago test markets Lite Beer in the Midwest. "Light" beers have been around since World War II, when brewers noticed that stateside women cut regular beer with water to make it taste better. Lite Beer was pretty much a flop . . . until the Miller Brewing Company purchased the rights to it in 1972 and started pumping millions of advertising dollars into it.

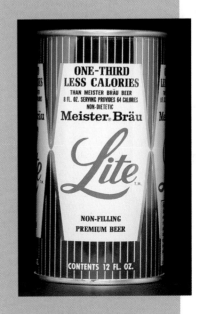

1968

The Maier Brewing Company in Los Angeles debuts "Old Vienna Beer," which contains the price right on the can—six for 87 cents. Some might consider this the nadir of American beer, but there's something special about the idea of getting a six-pack for less than a buck, no matter how awful the swill inside.

1969

Fritz Maytag (at left) buys the old Anchor Brewing Company in San Francisco. Maytag starts to brew his own iconoclastic version of beer for people who are tired of Bud and Miller. This sows the seeds of the microbrewery revolution.

1972

Oregon passes the first container deposit law. Finally, beer drinkers can get some return on their investment. (Certain states only; some restrictions apply.)

1977

Billy Carter, the gas station–owning brother of U.S. President Jimmy Carter, introduces his own beer. The can copy read: "I had this beer brewed just for me. I think it's the best I ever tasted. And I've tasted a lot. I think you'll like it, too." Breweriana collectors hoard cases of the stuff, thinking it'll be worth a lot of money someday. They are wrong. "You can barely give Billy Brew away," says Stan Galloway of *American Breweriana* magazine. "It's one of the biggest bombs in brewery history." Those 50-cent cans you could buy in '77 today are worth . . . 50 cents.

1978

Brewing beer at home is made legal in the United States, just as George Washington had intended more than 200 years ago. Within a few years, thousands of men will begin receiving Mr. Beer home-brewing kits for Christmas and Father's Day. For more information on brewing your own beer, see page 112.

1982

The first brewpub—Bert Grant's Yakima Brewing and Malting Company—opens in Yakima, Washington. This is the first time since Prohibition that a brewery is allowed to sell its own beer at its own bar. Within two years, brewpubs would be popping up all over the United States.

1993

The author turns 21 and retires with some close friends to the Sam Adams Brewhouse in Philadelphia. It is a Monday night, and glasses of sweet, nourishing Sammy are only a buck. The author drinks at least $11 worth of beer, and later can't remember how to spell his last name.

1994

Microbreweries—small operations producing non-mainstream beers, like Fritz Maytag did back in 1969—start to arrive in full force. In California alone, there are 84 new microbreweries—four more breweries than there were *nationally* in 1983.

2001

ONE NOT-SO-GREAT MOMENT

In the wake of the September 11 attacks, stories circulate about the "Bud Avenger," a hapless Budweiser delivery guy who stumbles upon two "Arabs" celebrating in their McFarland, California, convenience store. The delivery guy proceeds to remove every single Bud product from the store, then tells the workers never to call for a delivery again. This is clearly an urban legend; newspapers fail to find such a person, and Anheuser-Busch steadfastly denies the incident.

2003

People for the Ethical Treatment of Animals (PETA) lobbies Wisconsin Governor Jim Doyle to change the state's official beverage from milk to beer. PETA argues that beer is healthier than milk, which (it claims) has been linked to heart disease, cancer, allergies, diabetes, and obesity.

THE EVOLUTION OF THE BEER CAN

Why didn't ancient Egyptians store their beer in cold aluminum six-packs? Canned beer wasn't technically possible until the twentieth century. The problem was pressure. Wimpy canned liquids such as fruit juice require packaging that can withstand 25 to 35 pounds of pressure per square inch (1.8 to 2.5 kg/cm²); carbonated beer requires more than 80 pounds per square inch (5.6 kg/cm²). No matter how tough canneries made the cans, the beer would soon come bursting out at the seams. And that's no fun, unless your team has just won the Super Bowl.

But in 1933, the American Can Company solved the pressure problem by lining the inside of the cans with a special coating. The Gottfried Krueger Brewing Company in Newark, New Jersey, was the first brewery to give the newfangled cans a try. In late November 1933, Krueger shipped 2,000 cans of its "Special Beer" to its biggest customers, and asked them to fill out a short questionnaire. Ninety-one percent of the trial drinkers liked canned beer—and 85 percent said it tasted as good as beer straight from the tap. Canned beer was an immediate success.

Of course, that first can of Krueger was nothing like the beer cans that fill today's supermarket shelves. Back then, your beer came in . . .

FLAT TOPS: NOVEMBER 1933 TO CIRCA 1964

You haven't held a can of beer until you've held an old tin or steel can of beer (aluminum wasn't used for beer cans until 1959, when Coors introduced them). Cans used to weigh 4 ounces (114 g) each—and that's *without* the beer inside. Do some math, and you realize that a case of 24 *empty* cans weighed exactly 6 pounds (2.7 kg). Try sneaking *that* into the dorms. To make matters worse, you also needed an opener called a "church key" to puncture the tops. Still, beer in cans became wildly popular. So popular, in fact, that breweries without canning machinery began to feel left out. They came up with . . .

CONE TOPS: CIRCA 1935 TO 1960

The top was like a bottle, but the body was all metal. Although many brewers didn't have canning mechanisms, they did have the machinery required to stick caps on top of glass bottles. So, they simply ordered up a bunch of specially modified cans that could be topped like a bottle. There are four basic models of this unholy hybrid—low profile, high profile, j-spout, and the crowntainer—but all are essentially the same juglike can.

Returning World War II vets boosted sales of canned beer in the mid-1940s; after all, that's what they had been drinking overseas. Until the final days of the Kennedy administration, you drank your canned beer either in a flat top or a cone top. Then came a startling innovation that would change the beer world. . . .

Classic flat top cans (shown above): Hull's Cream Ale (1955); Straight Eight (1955); Pearl Lager (1952); Acme Beer (1950); Krueger's (1935); Yankee (1958); Esslinger (1958). Classic cone top cans (shown below): Hohenadel Light Beer (1940); Schlitz (1940); Esslinger's Little Man Ale (1940); Duquesne Can-o-Beer (1942); Neuweiler's Cream Ale (1947); Old German (1940); Sierra (1946).

Early pull tab cans (shown above): A-1 (1972); Guinness Extra Stout (1970); Orbit (1970); El Rancho (1972); Jaguar Malt Liquor (1965); Budweiser Budvar (1970); Keg Beer (1970). Modern stay tab cans (shown below): Sapporo (2000); Henri-Funck (1996); Foster's Lager (2000); Harley-Davidson Heavy Beer (1987); Thos Cooper and Sons (2000); Red Dog (1990); Yuengling Black & Tan (1999); Heineken (2000).

PULL TABS: MARCH 1963 TO CIRCA 1975

Pull tabs were a simple mechanism that allowed thirsty drinkers to put their fingers in a ring, pull, and—presto! A pie-wedge opening to fresh, cold beer. The first beer with a pull tab, Iron City Beer, debuted in 1963. That kicked off a pull-tab revolution: within two years, more than 70 percent of all cans would have pull tops. At last, any child with even rudimentary motor skills could open a beer. The only problem: those damned pull rings. Once those slivers of aluminum were yanked from the can, they were supposed to go right into the trash. Instead, they usually ended up on sidewalks and beaches and in people's feet. From the late 1960s to the early 1970s, pull tabs were a national menace. Then, finally, can engineers came up with . . .

STAY TABS: 1975 TO PRESENT

The tabs we're familiar with today. Same theory as a pull tab, only the wedge of aluminum is folded back into the can. No fuss, no cuts on your foot. Stay tabs became the standard for all canned beverages, not just beer. Sure, if you try hard enough, you can play with the tab until the metal wedge falls into the can. And yeah, theoretically, you can swallow it and die. But that's why you should *drink* a can of beer, not fiddle around with it.

OVERSIZED MONSTER CANS

The only other major beer-can innovation in the past 70 years has been one of size. At first, some beers came in 10-ounce (295-ml) cans. Eventually, 12 ounces (355 ml) became the standard. But in 1955, British brewers began to experiment with cans that held 16 ounces (470 ml)—a pint, in other words. Bigger was definitely better in the UK. The trend slowly traveled around the world, and today, many international favorites (Foster's, Sapporo, even Budweiser) are sold in 16-ounce, and sometimes 24-ounce (705 ml) cans. With oversized cans, you're facing a different kind of pressure problem: how cold your beer will stay depends on how fast you can drink it.

How to "Shotgun" a Beer

Do you absolutely, positively have to drink a can of beer in less than 3 seconds? It's time to pull out the shotgun.
1. Lay a can of beer on its side.
2. Puncture the can near the bottom with a house key.
3. Cover the puncture with your tongue and raise the beer to an upright position.
4. Pull the stay tab. The beer will now "shotgun" out of the puncture hole and, ideally, shoot past your teeth and down your throat. This works because air is rushing into the can through the top and forcing out the beer. It's up to you and your throat to keep up with it.

POPULAR EXPRESSIONS THAT CAME FROM BEER

Beer influences language, and not just in the way you think. ("Wasssat ossifer? You wanna see my lissens and regissration?") Many important English words and expressions originated at the bottom of a cold pint of ale. We can't possibly recount every single brilliant thought or turn of phrase inspired by beer, but here are some of the best.

BERSERK

In the middle of raping and pillaging yet another country, Vikings would often stop to drink huge quantities of *aul* (ale) by the bucket. Then they'd strip their armor and shirts and head back into battle topless. The Norse word *berserk* means "bare shirt," and eventually, "going berserk" would come to describe these beer-fueled bloodbaths. Today, at certain football games, you can still see fat white dudes going berserk, usually with logos painted on their not-so-Nordic chests.

BOOZE

A certain style of Egyptian beer was known as *boosa*, a word that soon warped into "booze." Ironically, booze came to describe all forms of liquor that were *not* beer.

HOBNOB

Way back in the Middle Ages, when you went to a tavern and spoke Old English, somebody would ask you: "Habbe or nabbe?" Literally, it meant: "Are you going to have a drink, or not?" Eventually, this phrase blurred into "hobnobbing," a synonym for socializing.

HONEYMOON

In ancient Babylonia, the father of a bride would supply his new son-in-law with a month's worth of mead, a honey beer. Since the calendar was based on phases of the moon, this month-long beer session came to be known as the "honey month," or "honeymoon."

JOE SIX-PACK

Beer marketers used this term to describe beer consumers during the early 1960s. The name soon replaced "John Q. Public" as denoting an ordinary workaday fellow.

LUNCHEON

In the Middle Ages, a liquid lunch was known as "nunchion," a combination of "noon scheken," or "noon drinking." Along with your beer, you would also enjoy a large chunk of bread, which was called "lunch" back then. Combine the two—in other words, have a hunk of bread and a pint of beer at your midday repast—and you'd be having a luncheon.

MIND YOUR P'S AND Q'S

"P's and Q's" is shorthand for pints and quarts, which is how the English take their beer. When customers in a pub got out of hand, the bartender would shout, "Mind yer pints and quarts!"

THE REAL MCCOY

Prohibition-era bootlegger Jim McCoy produced beer and liquors that were so close to real brands, they were known as "the real McCoy."

RULE OF THUMB

Adding yeast to beer mix is a tricky procedure. If the mix is too cold, the yeast won't have enough heat to grow. Too hot, and the yeast will burn up and die. But before brewers had fancy-schmancy tools like thermometers, they had to rely on the most basic of brewing tools: their own thumb. If the mix felt right, the yeast went in. This became known as the "rule of thumb."

SCOFFLAW

During Prohibition, law enforcement officials wanted a new name for people who ignored the law and drank alcohol anyway—something that would strike fear into the hearts of ordinary citizens. A Massachusetts millionaire named Delcevare King sponsored a contest in 1924 to establish the name and received more than 25,000 entries (the $200 first prize helped, but was measly by millionaires' standards). The winner: *scofflaw*. Oooh. We're shaking.

SCOT-FREE

In nineteenth-century England, beer drinkers in cities were expected to pay a tax called a "scot." Some chose to frequent rural, out-of-town bars instead, which meant they were able to drink "scot-free."

WET YOUR WHISTLE

Ever have trouble getting a bartender's attention? English drinkers came up with a novel solution to this problem decades ago. They'd take their favorite ceramic drinking mugs, then weld a whistle into the rim or handle. When it came time to fill up on more ale, the customer would simply "wet his whistle" to get the bartender's attention.

PRESTIGIOUS BEER AWARDS AND CEREMONIES

In days of old, people treated beer with extreme reverence. Trappist monks considered yeast nothing less than a divine miracle. Ancient Egypt got plastered in honor of Hathor, the Chief Goddess of Beer and "Queen of Drunkenness Without End." Nowadays, we pay homage to beer with the following rituals and ceremonies.

THE GREAT AMERICAN BEER FESTIVAL

Founded in 1981, this is the big one—the Oscars of the beer-brewing industry. Win a medal at this baby, and you can proudly adorn your can with it. Every year, close to 400 breweries show up to serve and brag about their beer, and the 21,000 people in attendance can choose from over 1,300 beers on tap. There are 91 judges drinking all of that beer—for official reasons, of course—and in exchange, they hand out 172 different medals in categories from Best Ale to Best Pilsner to Mid-Size Brewing Company of the Year. Attendees usually think they've died and gone to Beervana; the floor is organized like a giant map of the United States, so you can wander around different regions to sample the beers of that area. Paid attendees are given a special cup that entitles them to unlimited one-ounce samples of any beer at the festival. At that rate, you might never get out alive. For ticket info, check out www.beertown.org.

1-3: It doesn't get any better than this: Sipping and toasting at the Great American Beer Fesitval.

WORLD BEER GAMES

This is the beer equivalent of the Olympic Games, and while the events may sound a little frat boyish—"Quarters" and "Pint Chug" are two of the six official games—the founders take it very seriously. The proceedings are overseen by the "World Beer Games Sanctioning Body," which puts forth ethical codes and a complex set of rules and regulations. There's even a Latin motto: *Non Mihi, Non Tibi, Sed Cerevisia* ("Not for You, Not for Me, But for Beer"). Currently, 16 countries— Barbados, Belgium, Canada, the Dominican Republic, England, Greece, Guyana, Ireland, Italy, Jamaica, the Philippines, Poland, Portugal, South Korea, Trinidad and Tobago, and the United States—compete worldwide to prove "beer supremacy." My favorite event: the Recycling Can Toss, in which team members pitch 12-ounce (355-ml) aluminum cans into a recycling bin while seated in a recliner. For more game rules or sign-up information, go to www.worldbeergames.org. And be sure to check out the hilarious team profiles.

4. 2002 World Beer Games winners Team Canada—Paul Cesana, Tony Calderone, Scott Howe, Chris DeVries, and Brian Hill—celebrate with their trophy, the Brewers' Keg. 5. Ms. Pilsner, a contestant in the Miss World Beer Games Contest. 6. At the World Beer Games, Team Canada contestant Scott Howe prepares to go for the gold.

THE BEER DRINKER OF THE YEAR AWARD

Wynkoop Brewing Company started this award in 1997, and every year since it has flown three contestants to Denver, Colorado, to face a panel of nine black-robed, wigged judges, who hurl out endless beer trivia questions. Some questions are technical, some funny, some surreal. Sample questions include:

- What is hop traction?
- In the late 1950s, what cartoon character was used in advertising for Stag Beer?
- What would you do if the president installed you as Secretary of Beer?

After two hours of grilling, the last beer drinker standing is dubbed the "Beer Drinker of the Year," and receives free beer for life at the Wynkoop Brewery, $100 worth of beer at his/her favorite local brewpub, his/her name etched on a trophy at Wynkoop, and other "Beer Drinker of the Year" swag and apparel.

GUINNESS'S WIN YOUR OWN PUB IN IRELAND CONTEST

"Thanks for the pub."

There are so many pubs in Ireland, it's apparently no big deal to give one away every year. Guinness holds an annual contest to do just that. The competition begins at the local level—contestants have to submit an essay extolling the pleasures of the perfect pint of Guinness. A dozen of the best entries are chosen, and the writers are flown to Ireland to compete in a series of events, including dart-throwing, the ability to hold forth (i.e., bullshit in a bar), and last but not least, the ability to pull the perfect pint of Guinness. But the real fun ensues when the winner—always an American, since this is a United States–only contest—finds him-/herself the owner of a real pub in the middle of damp, old Ireland, with grumpy, craggy residents who don't like outsiders serving up their daily pints. Has anyone thought to make a sitcom about this contest?

ZULU BEER CEREMONY

If a member of the Zulu tribe approaches you with a beer and a knife, you're about to become a lifelong pal, as evidenced by a friendship ritual called Kasendi. It was observed by Dr. David Livingstone during the nineteenth century: "The Balonda have a most remarkable custom of cementing friendship. When two men agree to be special friends they go through a singular ceremony. The men sit opposite each other holding hands, and by the side of each is a vessel of beer. Slight cuts are then made on the clasped hands, on the pit of the stomach, on the right cheek, and on the forehead. The point of a grass-blade is pressed against each of these cuts, so as to take up a little of the blood, and each man washes the grass-blade in his own beer vessel. The vessels are then exchanged and the contents drunk, so that each imbibes the blood of the other. The two are thenceforth considered as blood-relations, and are bound to assist each other in every possible manner. While the beer is being drunk, the friends of each of the men beat on the ground with clubs, and bawl out certain sentences as ratification of the treaty. It is thought correct for all of the friends of each part to the contract to drink a little of the beer."

WORLD BEER RECORDS

Many people don't realize that the *Guinness Book of World Records* began as a humble guide to settling bar bets. In 1951, Sir Hugh Beaver, then the managing director of the Guinness Brewery, got into a sloppy argument over which European game bird flew the fastest—the grouse, or the golden plover? While resolving the debate, Sir Beaver realized that a book full of freaky bar trivia would fly off bookshelves faster than any stupid game bird, and he was right: More than 94 million copies of the Guinness Book have been sold since the first edition was released in August 1955. In honor of the Guinness book, we offer this shameless rip . . . er, small tribute.

WORLD'S STRONGEST BEER
SAMUEL ADAMS UTOPIAS

Mere mortal beers have an alcohol volume of anywhere from 5.4 to 9 percent; some light beers are as low as 2.4 to 5 percent. Utopias on the other hand is a liver-jolting *25 percent* alcohol. In the spirit world, this beer would be 50 proof. Each limited edition bottle—only 8,000 were brewed—will set you back $100.

WORLD'S WIMPIEST BEER
CATALINA BLONDE

Anheuser-Busch test-marketed this low-calorie, low-alcohol brew to appeal to people over 50 years old. Like many things marketed to senior citizens (denture cream, adult undergarments, *Matlock*), it is a matter of embarrassment.

HIGHEST PER CAPITA BEER CONSUMPTION (WORLD)
CZECH REPUBLIC

In 2002, the Czechs cancelled out an average of 159 liters of beer per person. The Irish came in second, at 125 liters per person. The U.S. ranked twelfth with a measley 84.4 liters per person.

Don't pound back six of *these* at the ballpark.

HIGHEST PER CAPITA BEER CONSUMPTION (UNITED STATES)
NEVADA

Beer lovers in Sin City's home state consume an average of 184 liters of beer per year. (Which is surprising, considering all of the free hard liquor you can get simply by standing next to a slot machine.)

SMALLEST PER CAPITA BEER CONSUMPTION
(UNITED STATES)
UTAH

Here, residents consume only 79 liters of beer per year. Then again, beer is scarce in this state, as beer lovers attending the 2002 Winter Olympic Games discovered.

Faced with countless bowling lanes, pool tables, and other distractions, patrons of the enormous Red's bar sometimes forget to drink their beer.

BIGGEST BAR
RED'S IN EDMONTON, ALBERTA, CANADA

This huge-ass bar Up North is 105,000 square feet (9,755 sq m) and can accommodate 2,000 customers. Good thing it can keep them busy with 28 bowling lanes, 24 pool tables, a nightclub, restaurant, two-level bar, and an arcade.

SMALLEST BAR
KENNY'S BAR IN THE QUEENS PUB IN CLEETHORPES, ENGLAND

Kenny's can only accommodate six customers in its 4-by-6 foot (1.2 x 1.8 m) space (although as many as 11 have squeezed in from time to time). To qualify as a "bar" in England, you have to serve booze and have a separate entrance to street level. So while technically Kenny's is part of a larger bar, the Queens Pub (in fact, Kenny's used to be the pub's storage closet), it has a separate entrance, qualifying it as a stand-alone establishment.

CREEPIEST BAR
THE FERRY BOAT INN IN HOLYWELL, ENGLAND
According to legend, this bar is haunted by the ghost of a teenage girl who hanged herself and then was buried in unconsecrated ground nearby. But that's not the creepy part. Years later, the bar expanded, and the girl's gravestone is now *inside* the bar.

BIGGEST BREWER
ANHEUSER-BUSCH
The makers of the "King of Beers" certainly rule the beer world. In 2002, A-B's worldwide sales reached an all-time high of 108.9 million barrels. Surprisingly, A-B's biggest seller isn't Bud, but Bud Light.

OLDEST BEER DRINKER
NJOKI WAINAINA
This Kenyan woman, 145 years old (or so her family claims), attributes her long life to a diet of bananas, maize, orange squash, and home-brewed beer. But since she doesn't have a birth certificate, you'd need a few beers before you're convinced her family is telling the truth.

BIGGEST BEER CAN
GUINNESS
Leave it to the brewer who invented the book to eventually make it *in* the book. On St. Patrick's Day 2002, the Guinness folks unveiled a 600-pound (272 kg) replica of an authentic Draught Guinness can—which could hold 3,608 liters of the delicious porter beer. It was 8,200 times the size of an ordinary draught can.

Shotgunning *this* beer could be fatal.

THE YEAR IN BEER

REASONS TO DRINK BEER ALL YEAR.

January 1: You had champagne out the wazoo last night. Time to settle your stomach with a nice quiet glass of beer while you watch the Rose Bowl.

January 5: Time for "Twelfth Night," the English holiday that requires wassailing—that is, the eating of spiced cakes and the drinking of vast amounts of beer.

The Monday After January 5: The English call this "Plough Monday," and it's a beer lover's version of Halloween. You're supposed to decorate a plow, then beg your neighbors for bread, cheese, and beer.

January 24: The first can of beer went on sale in Richmond, Virginia, in 1933.

February 22: Birthday of George Washington, noted beer brewer and Founding Father (see page 16).

March 17: St. Patrick's Day, a little-known Irish holiday.

April 6: On this night in 1933, Prohibition was lifted in 20 cities, including New York City, Washington, D.C., and San Francisco. Celebrated as "New Beer's Eve" by enthusiasts.

April 22: Happy Earth Day! Enjoy the planet's oldest fermented beverage.

May 3: The "Beer Barrel Polka" was recorded on this day in 1939 by the Andrews Sisters.

June 14: On this day in 1988, the Fat Boys sued Miller Brewing Company for using their likeness in a "Rapping Fats" Joe Piscopo beer commercial.

July 1–31: "American Beer Month," courtesy of the Association of Brewers.

September 8: The feast day of Saint Adrian, the Catholic patron saint of beer. He was born this day in A.D. 303.

October 6: On this day in 1880, the National League kicked out the Cincinnati Reds for selling beer at games.

November 8: Adolf Hitler tried to stage the infamous Munich Beer Hall Putsch and overthrow the German government in 1923.

November 15: America Recycles Day. Get to work generating those empty cans.

The Day Before the Super Bowl: Wynkoop Brewery in Colorado names its "Beer Drinker of the Year."	**Super Bowl Sunday:** The football is secondary.	**January 17:** Birthday of Benjamin Franklin, who once observed, "Beer is proof that God loves us."
March 19: Germany's *Fruhjahrsbierfest* ("early year beer festival"), a beer holiday held in honor of St. Joseph.	**Purim:** Jewish holiday of deliverance, and drinking.	**April 1:** Tell your significant other that drinking beer has been shown to cure cancer, enhance sexual performance, and eradicate static cling.
May 9: Joseph Bramah patents the beer pump handle on this day in 1785.	**Memorial Day:** Thousands of men died so you could enjoy that beer free from tyranny or oppression. Do 'em proud.	**June 4:** The Cleveland Indians held "Ten Cent Beer Night" on this night in 1974, but had to forfeit to the Texas Rangers after drunk fans got out of control.
September 16: Mayflower Day. Remember: America was founded because of a beer run. Plymouth was chosen because of stinginess (see page 16).	**Sunday Before October 2:** Tap-Up Day, a medieval holy day in Guilford, England, when anyone could sell beer without a license.	**First Sunday in October:** The last day of Oktoberfest, (a 16-day extravaganza for beer lovers). Remember to thank Prince Ludwig and Princess Theresa (see page 18).
December 5: Prohibition ended across the nation on this day in 1933 (see page 23). Raise a glass to the 21st Amendment.	**December 25:** Christmas. Ask Santa for membership in a Beer of the Month club.	**December 26–28:** Feast of Fools, a medieval celebration held in a church, where a mock priest would preach to a drunken crowd, some of whom would wear donkey masks and shout back obscene jokes.

E ATLAS OF BEER

"For any country to be a country, you have to have an air force, a
football team, and a beer. You can get by without the air force and
the football team, but you have to have a beer."—*Frank Zappa*

We are all beer explorers. At first, the world of beer seems small—its borders are within Dad's beer fridge, and consist of whatever we can swipe without him noticing. As we grow older, we grow more courageous, seeking out bolder and more exotic beers. We embrace regional microbrews and specially imported beers from across oceans. And with maturity we realize that the beer universe is as vast as the starry sky.

Over the next few pages, we'll take a guided tour of the world of beer. First, we'll stop in Europe, the undisputed top beer continent, to sample Czech pilsners and Belgian ales and English bitters. Then we'll hop over the Pond to see what the Yanks and their microbreweries are up to. Finally, we'll zip around the globe to see what a few other countries are keeping on tap. Please have your passports ready, and return your trays to the upright and locked position.

MAP KEY

	CAN'T-MISS BREWERY TOUR		PROMINENT HOPS-GROWING REGION
	CAN'T-MISS BAR, PUB, OR BEER GARDEN		PROMINENT BARLEY-GROWING REGION

IRELAND

Don't believe the pub is the center of Irish social life? There are more than 1,000 of them within the city limits of Dublin alone. And the literary town of Listowel, in County Kerry, has one pub for every eight residents. The national beer, of course, is Guinness, and you really haven't had it until you've ordered a pint in Ireland. If you find yourself in a Gaelic-speaking pub, say, "Is fearr liom beoir" ("I prefer beer").

LEGAL DRINKING AGE: 18

NUMBER OF BREWERIES: 13

HOW TO SAY "CHEERS": "Slainte!"
(pronounced slawncha)

NATIVE BEERS: Guinness (a), Harp (b), Beamish Irish Stout (c), Murphy's Irish Stout (d), Smithwicks Ale (e)

BELFAST ★

IRELAND

ISL
M

GALWAY

DUBLIN ★ ⓐ ⓒ

IRISH

ⓒ
KILKENNY •

ⓒ ⓓ
CORK •

CELTIC SEA

Cooke's Thatch Bar (Galway). The same family has owned this pub for six generations, and they're kind enough to let you lounge in the beer garden, use the barbecue, or even tickle the ivories, if you're so inclined.

The Guinness Brewery (Dublin). It's Ireland's version of Disneyland. The tour is self-guided, so you can rush through the audio-visual presentations and head straight for the sampling bar, where your price of admission covers two pints.

Stag's Head (Dublin). Want to see a pub preserved the way it was 100 years ago, with the original mahogany bar and stained-glass windows? Ask a Dubliner to direct you to 1 Dame Court, off of Dame Lane.

THE UNITED KINGDOM: ENGLAND, SCOTLAND, AND WALES

"Pub" is shorthand for the English term "public house." Many Americans dream of visiting a public house to taste the warm beer, but this is a myth—the English don't necessarily drink their beer warm. It's just warmer than all the American beers that are served ice-cold (some wags claim that this helps distinguish it from urine).

● ORKNEY

COTLAND

★ EDINBURGH

ⓘ ● NEWCASTLE UPON TYNE

LEGAL DRINKING AGE: 18. British law also says that alcohol may be consumed starting at age 5, with parental consent.

NUMBER OF BREWERIES: More than 450

HOW TO SAY "CHEERS": In England, it's "Cheers!"; in Wales, say, "lechyd da!" (pronounced yecheeda); in Scotland, say, "Slainte!" (pronounced slawncha) or "Here's tae ye!"

NATIVE BEERS: Fuller's (f), Young's (g), Bass Pale Ale (h), Newcastle Brown Ale (i), McEwan's No. 1 Champion Ale (j), Orkney Skullsplitter (k)

ENGLAND

ⓗ ● BURTON ON TRENT

Fuller's Griffin Brewery (London). The tour showcases the elaborate brewing process from the malt silo to the grist case to the fermenting vessel to kegging and bottling. Naturally, pints of Fuller's are provided at tour's end.

LES

THAMES RIVER

★ CARDIFF   LONDON ★ ⓕ ⓖ

Gordon's (London's West End). Believed to be one of London's oldest continually operating pubs. Also check out Public Life in the heart of London, which is actually a beer bar in a giant ... well, tiled loo. (DJs love the place because of the excellent acoustics.)

ENGLISH CHANNEL

AVERAGE ANNUAL BEER CONSUMPTION IN LITERS

Ireland 125
UK 95

| 0 | 25 | 50 | 75 | 100 | 125 | 150 |

BELGIUM

Belgium is the most beer-crazy country on Earth; it's barely the size of Maryland, yet over 100 brewers produce 650 different types of beer. Many beer enthusiasts fly to Belgium just to hit one of the four major beer cities—Brussels, Antwerp, Gent, and Brugge—and hop from bar to bar, trying wild varieties of Trappist ales, lambics, aged beers, and everything else they could only dream about in their home country.

WADDEN ISLANDS

LEGAL DRINKING AGE: **15**

NUMBER OF BREWERIES: **110**

HOW TO SAY "CHEERS": **"Op uw gezonheid!"** (pronounced op uv ga ZON hite)

NATIVE BEERS: **Cantillion Kriec Lambic (a), Hoegaarden (b), Duvel (c), Leffe (d), Westvleteren (e)**

AMSTERDAM

Kulminator (Antwerp). This slightly hard-to-find bar in downtown Antwerp stocks an amazing 650 varieties of bottled beer, including beer that is no longer produced and rare, temperature-controlled beers that were stocked back in the early 1970s, when the bar opened.

BREDA • ⓙ

• BRUGGE

• ANTWERP
• BREENDONK

GHENT •
• WESTVLETEREN

ⓒ ⓑ

ⓐ ★ BRUSSELS

• LEUVEN

Interbrew (Leuven). Interbrew, the makers of Stella Artois and one of the biggest brewers in the world, lets you watch the master brewers at work and taste-test the fruits of their labors.

BELGIUM

ⓓ • DIN.

Brasserie Cantillion (Brussels). One of the few places in the world you'll ever see lambic beer brewed—a process that involves wild yeasts—in 100-year-old red copper vats.

Bier Circus (Brussels). The name says it all—this world-famous Belgian brew mecca has a beer menu that's as thick as a small-town phone directory.

THE NETHERLANDS

One thing to know when ordering beer in the Netherlands: the sizes are small. Ask for a glass of beer, and you'll get something that more closely resembles a shot glass than a pint. You can ask for *een beir groot*, which will be bigger, but definitely not pint-sized. Still, there's a good reason for the beer being small: it packs a more serious alcohol punch that the beers you're probably used to, including familiar favorites like Heineken. Most exports are watered down for wimpy foreigners.

THE
ETHERLANDS

LEGAL DRINKING AGE: None (but to purchase beer, you must be 16)

NUMBER OF BREWERIES: 60

HOW TO SAY "CHEERS": "Proost!" or "Gezondhied" (translation: "To your health")

NATIVE BEERS: Budels (f), Heineken (g), Amstel Light (h), Grolsch Premium Lager (i), Oranjeboom Premium Lager (j), Wieckse Witte (k)

Heineken (Amsterdam). Tours occur throughout the day, but make sure you weasel your way into the first one. There's a tradition that the first group to complete the tour is rewarded with an hour's worth of free beer in the on-site pub.

Café In de Wildman (Amsterdam) is unique for two reasons: it's one of the few smoke-free bars in Amsterdam, and there's never any music blaring, so you can actually enjoy your small Dutch beers with some audible conversation. Seventeen local brews on tap, with 200 bottled selections.

Café 't Arendsnest (Amsterdam) makes a point of only serving beer that is brewed in the Netherlands, as opposed to many other cafés in town, that specialize in Belgian beers. At any given time, there are about 350 varieties available, including 250 seasonal types.

AVERAGE ANNUAL BEER CONSUMPTION IN LITERS

Belgium 99						
Netherlands 85						
0	25	50	75	100	125	150

GERMANY & AUSTRIA

GERMANY

The heart of the German beer experience, of course, is the traditional beer garden. Before refrigeration, lager beer had to ferment in cold underground cellars. Some breweries would build chestnut tree gardens on top of those cellars, and these would be extremely cool and pleasant places to be during the summer. Many beer garden names still end in *keller*, which is German for "cellar." Beer gardens are only open in the warm weather; when they close, everyone shuffles off to the nearby beer halls.

> LEGAL DRINKING AGE: **16 for beer and wine; 18 for spirits**
>
> NUMBER OF BREWERIES: **More than 1,250**
>
> HOW TO SAY "CHEERS": **"Prosit!" or "Stoss an!"** (translation: "Clink glasses")
>
> NATIVE BEERS: **Beck's (a), DAB Traditional (b), Bitburger Premium Pilsner (c), Erdinger Weissbräu (d)**

CAN'T-MISS BEER GARDENS:

No lederhosen required. But you might want to bring your own food; many traditional beer gardens don't supply much more than snacks. If there's no tablecloth, you'll have to fetch your own beer. If there is a tablecloth, expect to be served. Speaking of which, it's customary to tip your servers at least 10 percent, which you'll want to do, since they're typically extremely attentive to your beer needs. One last thing: Don't insult your server by asking for a "small" glass of beer. He's going to bring you at least a half-liter, and you'll drink it, damn it.

Löwenbräukeller (Munich). Over 1,800 seats, and they're usually jammed. But it's worth the wait. When you spot an open seat, ask, "Gestatten?" ("Is this seat free?") before you park your butt. While you're in Munich, you might also try the Augustinerkeller and the Salvatorkeller.

NORTH SEA

BREMEN •   ⓐ

GERMANY

• DORTMUND
ⓑ

RHINE RIVER

RHINE VALLEY

ⓒ
• BIT

THE BLACK FOREST

AUSTRIA

British politician David Lloyd George once said, "We are fighting Germany, Austria, and drink, and as far as I can see, the greatest of these three deadly foes is drink." George was always a bit of a stick-in-the-mud, but he was onto something in linking Germany and Austria with luscious, tempting drink. Austria has always played the slightly homely younger sister to Germany in the beer world, but the comparison is unfair—the country's state of Oberösterreich produces Märzens, lagers, and pilsners to rival those of Bavaria, just across the border. And Austrian native son Arnold Schwarzenegger said it best when he said that "milk is for babies—real men drink beer."

LEGAL DRINKING AGE: 16 for beer and wine; 18 for spirits

NUMBER OF BREWERIES: 88

HOW TO SAY "CHEERS": "Prosit!" or "Stoss an!" (translation: "Clink glasses")

NATIVE BEERS: Augustiner Marzen (e), Kaltenhausen Edelweiss (f), Eggenberger Urbock 23 (g), Goesser (h)

Schweizerhaus (Vienna). Open until midnight—most beer gardens fold up around 10 or 10:30—and famous for its authentic Budweiser Budvar, the German version, not the American macro version.

Augustinerbräu Kloster Mülln (Salzburg). In the site of a former monastery, this beer hall near Mozart's hometown includes a small market in the front to buy classic Austrian bar snacks (sausages, bread) and a self-serve bar where you can save money by pouring your own pitchers.

BALTIC SEA

LBE RIVER

★ BERLIN

DANUBE RIVER

(d) • ERDING
• MUNICH

VIENNA ★

AUSTRIA

SALZBURG •

(e)(f)   (h) • LOEBEN
            • OBERÖSTERREICH
            (g)

THE ALPS

AVERAGE ANNUAL BEER CONSUMPTION IN LITERS

Germany 127
Austria 108

0 | 25 | 50 | 75 | 100 | 125 | 150

THE CZECH REPUBLIC

If it weren't for two small cities in the Czech Republic (formerly Bohemia, and more recently part of Czechoslovakia), beer as we know it would be forever changed. The city of Pilsen gave us pilsner beer—90 percent of the beer in the world—and the city of Budweis gave us Budweiser, which sometimes seems like 90 percent of the pilsners in the world. There is a Czech urban legend that drinking beer helps you live longer because it reduces the aluminum (!?) in your body. Of course, life expectancy in the Czech Republic is the lowest of any country in Europe, so we might take this advice with a grain of salt.

LEGAL DRINKING AGE: 18

NUMBER OF BREWERIES: 80

HOW TO SAY "CHEERS": "Na zdravi!"
(pronounced nahz DRAH vee.
Translation: "To your health")

NATIVE BEERS: Gambrinus (a), Pilsner Urquell (b), Czech Rebel (c), Herold (d), Budwesier Budvar (e)

Ungelt Jazz & Blues Club (Prague). Here you can sample Czech classics such as Pilsner Urquell straight from the tap in the subterranean cellars dating back to the fifteenth century—pretty much when Urquell was first brewed.

Visit Pilsen (near Prague). The birthplace of pilsner-style beer. There, you can tour the Plzensky Prazdroj Brewery, the brewers of Pilsner Urquell.

COOL FACT: Hops were cultivated in the area as far back as A.D. 859, and historians have discovered evidence of beer being brewed here as early as 1088. Former Bohemian King Wenceslas ordered the death penalty for anybody caught smuggling precious hops out of the country.

BALTIC SEA

ZYW

ODER RIVER

WROC

ELBE RIVER

PRAGUE
(a)(b) (c) • BROD
• PILSEN CZECH
(d) • BREZNICE REPUBL
• CESKE BUDEJOVICE
(e)

POLAND

You can find beer almost anywhere in Poland, but it won't always be served cold. Be sure to ask for *zimne piwo* (cold beer). Polish pubs tend to be darkly lit, if lit at all. This could be a holdover from the days when you had to hide your bars and pubs from Communist rule, or perhaps even from when you had to hide your bars and pubs from invading Germans during the Second World War. Most Polish beer tends to be of the pale lager variety, but there is a distinctive Polish beer style called *grodziske*, which is a top-fermenting smoked wheat beer produced by a brewery in Grodzisk.

⑨
● ELBAG

Ⓗ Ⓘ
● BIALYSTOK

BUG RIVER

ULA RIVER

★ WARSAW

POLAND

KRAKOW ●

CARPATHIAN MOUNTAINS
Ⓚ ● BRZESKO

LEGAL DRINKING AGE: None, but you must be 18 to buy beverages that are more than 4.5 percent alcohol. Weaker alcoholic beverages—including many beers—can be purchased by anyone.

NUMBER OF BREWERIES: 80

HOW TO SAY "CHEERS": "Na Zdrowie!" (pronounced naz DRO vee ah. Translation: "To your health.")

NATIVE BEERS: Zywiec (f), Hevelius (g), Dojlidy (h), Zubr (i), Piast (j), Okocim (k)

Nora Pub (Warsaw). It has 14 local beers on tap, and looks sort of like a grade-school cafeteria, which only adds to its appeal.

Fischer Pub (Krakow). The sign on the door says "Members Only," but don't let that dissuade you—they don't turn anyone away. Inside, you'll find Zywiec on tap and a friendly, relaxed crowd.

COOL FACT: In 1845, there were over 1,100 breweries in Poland. On the eve of World War II, there were 144.

AVERAGE ANNUAL BEER CONSUMPTION IN LITERS

Czech Republic 159		
Poland 40		

| 0 | 25 | 50 | 75 | 100 | 125 | 150 |

* see page 37

SCANDINAVIA

Something's also fermenting in the state of Denmark . . . and in its Scandinavian neighbors, Norway, Sweden, and Finland. The annual highlight for beer-loving folks in Nordic countries is the Stockholm Beer Festival, during which 250,000 or so drinkers plow through 340 types of beer in four days. Michael Jackson has claimed this is probably one of the four most important beer fests in the world—and a personal favorite. That alone would be reason enough to book a trip now, but there's other cool beer lore to explore in this part of the world.

NORWAY

Norwegians have been drinking beer for a long time; in ancient Norse graves, archeologists have found cups and the remains of beer. Norway's Gulating Law, dating back to A.D. 1000, details when and how beer should be brewed at home.

> LEGAL DRINKING AGE: 18
>
> NUMBER OF BREWERIES: 16
>
> HOW TO SAY "CHEERS": "Skal!" (pronounced skoll)
>
> NATIVE BEERS: Aass Bock, Classic and Pilsner (a)

Aass Brewery (Drammen). A real Norwegian Viking would pronounce it "ouse," but after touring this country's oldest brewery, you'll be bragging to friends back home that you had plenty of you-know-what on your vacation.

DENMARK

The Danes are probably the biggest beer fans in Scandinavia; there's a lively group called the Danish Beer Enthusiasts (www.ale.dk) whose mission is to promote the beers of their homeland.

> LEGAL DRINKING AGE: 15 (but you must drink off premises until you're 18)
>
> NUMBER OF BREWERIES: 15
>
> HOW TO SAY "CHEERS": "Skal" (pronounced skoll)
>
> NATIVE BEERS: Carlsberg (b), Elephant (c)

SWEDEN

NORWAY

★ OSLO
• DRAMMEN
(a)

STOCKHOL

(h)
• GÖTEBORG

DENMARK

NORTH SEA

(b) (c)
COPENHAGEN ★

Carlsberg (Copenhagen). Tours of this enormous brewery (see page 89) are offered twice a day. Watch for a pair of stone elephants at the entrance gate, guarding the precious stores of beer.

	0	25	50	75	100	125	150
Norway 52							
Sweden 59							
Finland 79.9							
Denmark 102							

FINLAND

A traditional Finnish drink is *sahti*, a wheat-based cousin of beer that was served at weddings and other special occasions. Tradition is nice, but these days, most Finns drink tastier, more modern brews.

LEGAL DRINKING AGE: **18**

NUMBER OF BREWERIES: **3**

HOW TO SAY "CHEERS": **"Kippis!"** (pronounced kip-iSS)

NATIVE BEERS: Olvi Special (d), Koff Jouluolut (e), Synebrychoff (f), Lapin Kulta (g)

FINLAND

(d) • LISALMI

(e) (f)
KERAVA•
(g) ★ HELSINKI

Atelier (Helsinki). It's on top of one of the city's tallest buildings. The views are the best you'll ever see while clutching a beer. And don't forget to check beneath your butt as you sip your Lapin Kulta: Those barstools were designed by Aalto, a famed Finnish designer.

SWEDEN

Swedish beer is like Ikea furniture—functional, simple, and nothing to write home to Mom about. Still, Swedish beer history stretches back to the Vikings, who drank mead and proceeded to rampage like characters in *The Lord of the Rings* trilogy. (See page 13.)

IC SEA

The Ice Bar (Stockholm). The closest you'll ever come to entering Superman's Fortress of Solitude. All patrons are required to wear coats and hats. The interior temperature feels like it is set to "meat locker," and everything—the tables, the seats, even the very beer glasses—are crafted from cold slabs of ice. Seriously.

LEGAL DRINKING AGE: **18**

NUMBER OF BREWERIES: **34**

HOW TO SAY "CHEERS": **"Skal!"** (pronounced skoll)

NATIVE BEERS: Carnegie Stark Porter (h)

WESTERN EUROPE

Beer isn't exactly the first beverage that comes to mind when you mention any of these countries, but that's an oversight. There's nothing more refreshing than an ice-cold Italian beer on a hot day in Milan. While it's true that most Mediterranean countries prefer a vastly inferior alcoholic beverage called "wine," beer is slowly making inroads in all of these nations.

PORTUGAL

Don't mistake this beer-loving country for a suburb of Spain! Ask for beer that's *fresco* (cool) or it may be served *natural* (room temperature). Visit Lisbon in June to enjoy the beers at countless open-air street festivals.

> LEGAL DRINKING AGE: There is no minimum drinking age.
>
> NUMBER OF BREWERIES: 10
>
> HOW TO SAY "CHEERS": "A sua saude" (pronounced ah SOO-ah sah-OHH-day)
>
> NATIVE BEERS: Super Bock (a), Sagres (b)

Cervejas Sagres (downtown Lisbon). Makers of Sagres, the country's #1 brew.

SPAIN

Spain's Emperor Charles V (1500-1558) was a beer lover; one of the first laws he passed as Emperor was a beer purity law.

> LEGAL DRINKING AGE: 16
>
> NUMBER OF BREWERIES: 22
>
> HOW TO SAY "CHEERS": "Salud!" (pronounced sah-LOOD)
>
> NATIVE BEERS: Cruzcampo (c), Ambar Especial (d), Negra (e)

Cerveceria Santa Barbara (Madrid). A beer-only bar dating back to 1815 that also offers an outstanding array of tapas.

SEINE R

PARIS

LOIRE RIVER

BAY OF BISCAY

FRANCE

PORTUGAL

EBRO RIVER

PYRENEES MOUNTAINS

ZARAGOZA • (d)

LISBON

(a) (b)

TAGUS RIVER

MADRID

(e)

MARSEILLE

SPAIN

MEDITERRANEAN

SEVILLE • (c)

FRANCE

The French are crazy about their wines, but there are still a large number of citizens dedicated to beer making, especially in the Nord-Pas de Calais and Alsace-Lorraine regions.

The Cave de Gambrinus (Mulhouse). It features a selection of at least 30 French beers.

NCHIN
FONTAINE
HORDAIN

MULHOUSE

THE ALPS

AZZATE

UDINE • ⓚ

ITALY

PISA •

APPENNINE MOUNTAINS

ⓙ ★ ROME

ITALY

Most Italians look at beer as a novelty—they drink very little of it, compared to gallons of wine. Still, if it weren't for the few Italian breweries, American beer snobs wouldn't have anything to drink with their pizza.

COOL BREWERY SCHOOL: The Universitá della Birra (Azzate) was founded by an Italian journalist interested in teaching pub owners and would-be brewers the art of beer making.

Fiddler's Elbow (Rome). Dozens of English- and Irish-style pubs have infiltrated Rome in recent years, and Fiddler's Elbow is the granddaddy of them all. If you're desperate for a pint of Guinness—or to mingle with other tourists—this is the place to go.

AVERAGE ANNUAL BEER CONSUMPTION IN LITERS

	0	25	50	75	100	125	150
Italy 29.2							
France 38.7							
Spain 72							
Portugal 64.3							

American beer eerily mirrors American foreign policy: it's everywhere, yet nobody seems to like it very much. The British, in particular, have had a good old time mocking American beer, starting with the Monty Python joke about why American beer is like having sex in a canoe. (Answer: Because it's fucking near water.)

But if it's the exotic and unusual you want in your beer, you don't have to leave U.S. borders. Microbreweries have exploded over the past 20 years, producing a vast array of beers for every possible taste. Here, then, is a quick-and-dirty beer tour of the continental USA, starting with New England.

VERMONT

Three Needs Brewery and Taproom (Burlington). Besides brewing its own Belgian dubbels, smoke beers and other nontraditional brews, it also runs a *Simpsons*-themed happy hour six days a week.

NATIVE BEERS: Magic Hat Brewery (South Burlington) is the most whimsical brewer in all of New England. Its "artifactory" (brewery) produces ales and lagers with names such as Ale of the Living Dead, Fat Angel (pale ale), Heart of Darkness (stout), Chaotic Chemistry (barley wine–style), and Thumbsucker (stout).

CONNECTICUT

The Willimantic Brewing Company (Willimantic). Its life began in the old lobby and concession stand of a shuttered movie theater; it has since expanded to a spacious former U.S. Post Office building and serves the only postal-themed brews in the country, including Mail Order Old Ale and Address Unknown IPA.

BURLINGTON
SOUTH BURLINGTON
MONTPELIER
MT. WASHINGTON
VERMONT
NEW HAMPSHIRE
PORTLAN
CONCORD
PORTSMOUTH
CONNECTICUT RIVER
SOMERVILLE
BOSTON
MASSACHUSETTS
RHODE ISLAND
PROVIDENC
CONNECTICUT
HARTFORD
WILLIMANTIC
WAKEF
APP

MAINE

Gritty McDuff's (Portland). The first post-Prohibition brewpub in the state. Gritty's serves up some nice seasonal brews such as Halloween Ale and Vacationland Summer Ale. There's another Gritty's in Freeport.

MAINE

NATIVE BEER: Shipyard Export Ale (Portland) is brewed on the site of three former nineteenth-century shipyards. And Geary's Pale Ale (Portland) has a very cool label with a fat-ass lobster. If that doesn't say Maine, what does?

GUSTA

NEW HAMPSHIRE

NATIVE BEER: Smuttynose Brewing (Portsmouth) is probably the top microbrewer in New Hampshire. It's named after an island off the coast that was the scene of some grisly murders in 1873, but it's not all doom and gloom. Its weizen beer, Smuttynose Weizenheimer, has the goofiest name in all of beerdom.

ATLANTIC OCEAN

MASSACHUSETTS

RedBones Barbecue (Somerville). If you can't decide which beer you'd like to try, the bartender will spin a wheel and decide for you.

NATIVE BEER: Samuel Adams (Boston). The first batch of Sammy was brewed by founder Jim Koch in his own kitchen. Today, however, most of it is contract-brewed elsewhere.

RHODE ISLAND

The Mews Tavern (Wakefield). The number of microbrews on tap (69) makes it feel bigger than the state itself.

Now we move to the no-nonsense Mid-Atlantic, from the storied saloons of lower Manhattan to America's oldest continuously operating brewery to beachside pints on the shores of Delaware to the pinstriped beer dens of the nation's capital.

PENNSYLVANIA

Yuengling (Pottsville). America's oldest continuously operating brewery. For years, Yuengling was a cheapie coal miner's favorite; now, it's one of the most popular beers in the Mid-Atlantic, giving even Bud a run for its money. The tour culminates in a trip to the floor bottling plant, where hundreds of capped, washed, and filled bottles will whiz by your head in a Yuengling fever dream.

NATIVE BEER: The Victory Brewing Company (Downingtown) has created microbrews that have caused a national stir among beer geeks. Such success was a long time in the making. Victory's founders—Bill Covaleski and Ron Barchet—met when they were 10 years old.

Yard's Brewing Company (Philadelphia). It's located in the old Weissbrod & Hess Brewing Company building.

MARYLAND

NATIVE BEER: Try the Baltimore Brewing Company's DeGroen's Pils. Their beer logos are adorned with the image of Duke Gambrinus, a medieval leader from Antwerp who is considered a "spiritual patron of great beer."

WASHINGTON, D.C.

Kramerbooks/Afterwords (Washington, D.C.) is a combination bookstore/brewpub, which is probably the greatest mixture since your peanut butter fell into my chocolate. (Plus, Monica Lewinsky shopped here.)

The Brickskeller (Washington, D.C.) has more than 1,000 varieties of bottled beer available at all times.

NEW YOR

PENNSYLVANIA

HARRISBURG ★

MARYLAN

BALTIMO

ANNAPOLIS

WASHINGTON, D.C. ★

MID-ATLANTIC

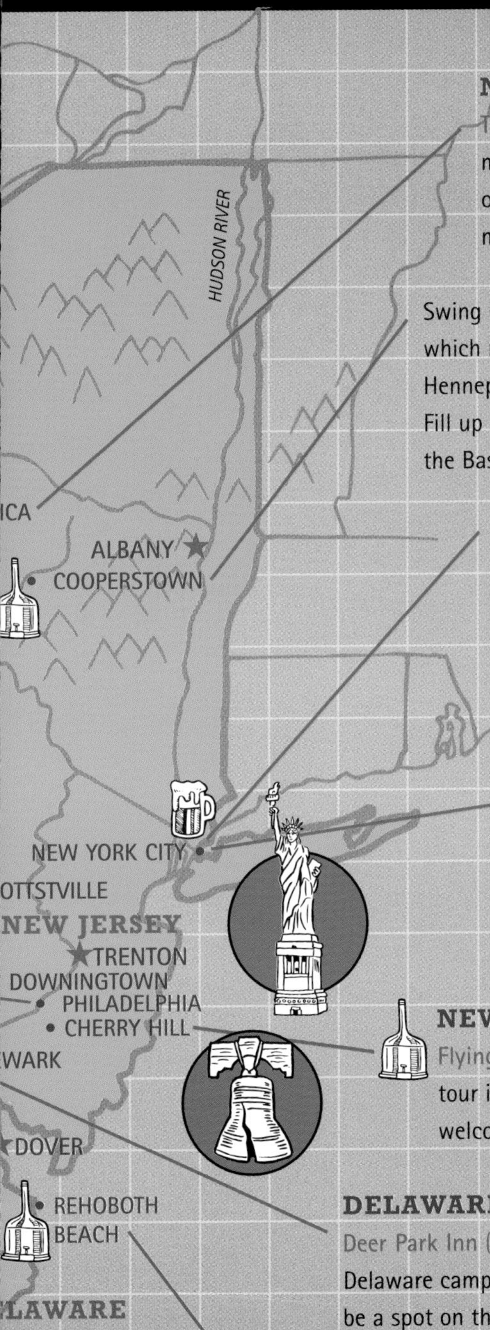

NEW YORK

The F. X. Matt Brewing Company (Utica). The maker of Utica Club and the Saranac brands offers a hands-on tour that allows you to feel the malted barley and hops used to brew their beers.

Swing by Cooperstown and visit Brewery Ommegang, which makes authentic Trappist beers such as Hennepin, Rare Vos, Snail Pale, and Three Philosophers. Fill up on these heavy, hearty ales, then head over to the Baseball Hall of Fame.

McSorley's Old Ale House (New York City). A men-only bar founded in 1854 with the motto, "Good ale, raw onions, and no ladies," McSorley's was finally forced to admit women in 1970 after being threatened with legal action. But to this day, there's only one bathroom.

Rheingold (New York City) was best known in the 1950s for its annual Miss Rheingold competition; now, both the beer and contest have made a comeback. (See page 176.)

NEW JERSEY

Flying Fish Brewing Company (Cherry Hill). A free tour includes samples of their beer. Kids are even welcome, if they're "well-behaved."

DELAWARE

Deer Park Inn (Newark). This bar, near the University of Delaware campus, is cool for three reasons: 1. The site used to be a spot on the Underground Railroad. 2. According to legend, there is one of the original markers of the Mason-Dixon Line in the basement. 3. Edgar Allan Poe allegedly put a curse on the inn after he fell in some mud outside.

Dogfish Head Brews and Eats (Rehoboth Beach). In the summer it offers "Pints and Paddles"—a combination brewery tour/kayak trip.

Map labels: HUDSON RIVER, ICA, ALBANY, COOPERSTOWN, NEW YORK CITY, OTTSVILLE, NEW JERSEY, TRENTON, DOWNINGTOWN, PHILADELPHIA, CHERRY HILL, WARK, DOVER, REHOBOTH BEACH, LAWARE

Next, we hop down South to a land of extremes. This terrain manages to include both the capital of American boozing (New Orleans) as well as a vast beer wasteland (pretty much the entire state of Mississippi). You might want to travel with a cooler full of cold ones, just in case . . .

ARKANSAS

NATIVE BEER: The Ozark Brewing Company (Little Rock) is a huge, cavernous brewpub with pine floors, cherrywood furniture, and beers such as Six in Hand Stout and Clara the Fair, a pale ale.

MISSISSIPPI

This is the only one of the 50 states to never have a brewery—micro or otherwise. Get with the program, Mississippi!

LOUISIANA

NATIVE BEERS: Abita Brewing Company (Abita Springs) is one of the original craft breweries in the South, founded in 1986. Try an Abita Amber.

At the Dixie Brewing Company (New Orleans), you have to try the Dixie Blackened Voodoo, a dark and hoppy witch's brew. Avoid the Dixie White Moose like a bad curse.

The Crescent City Brewhouse (New Orleans). The only brewpub in the French Quarter, serving brew since 1991. It's the perfect place to escape the Hurricane madness that seems to dominate this town.

ALABAMA

NATIVE BEER: The Montgomery Brewing Company (Montgomery) was one of the first to open after Alabama passed a microbrew law that allowed such institutions to exist. Stop in and try a sampler size of each of their beers— Wipe Out Stout, Old Montgomery Blonde, and Goat Hill Pale Ale—for only 75 cents a pop.

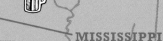

LEXINGTON
KENTUC
ARKANSAS
★ NASH
TENNESSEE
★ LITTLE ROCK
ALABAM
MISSISSIPPI
MONTGOMERY ★
LOUISIANA MISSISSIPPI RIVER ★ JACKSON
BATON ROUGE
★ ABITA SPRINGS • PENS
NEW ORLEANS

THE SOUTH

VIRGINIA

The Old Dominion Brewing Company (Ashburn), workin' the wort since 1990 in the D.C. area, brews Tuppers' Hop Pocket Pils and Dominion Lager. It celebrated its ten-thousandth batch of beer with a special Belgian-style tripel dubbed "Dominion Maniacs."

NORTH CAROLINA

NATIVE BEER: Weeping Radish Brewing Company (Roanoke Island) is a traditional Bavarian brewery located on the Outer Banks. Try their Hefeweizen and Fest beers.

Old Hickory Brewing Company (Hickory). The booths are made from giant wine barrels. (The only way to make this cooler is to have booths made out of giant beer barrels.)

GEORGIA

NATIVE BEER: Red Brick Beer (Atlanta) has an interesting story behind its name. The owner of the original Atlanta Brewing Company (dating back to the 1800s) suffered many setbacks over the years, the worst of which was a devastating brewery fire that consumed his wooden building. "This brewery will be rebuilt!" he vowed. "And this time, it will be constructed from strong red brick!" In 1994, the newly formed Atlanta Brewing Company decided to honor this tenacity on every bottle of beer.

FLORIDA

McGuire's Irish Pub (Pensacola). It adheres to the credo "Feasting, imbibery, and debauchery," and it's hard to argue with that kind of thinking. Instead of a Blarney Stone, it's considered good luck to kiss the head of a stuffed moose on the wall.

Map labels

WEST VIRGINIA
★ CHARLESTON
ASHBURN •
RICHMOND ★
VIRGINIA

ROANOKE ISLAND •
NORTH CAROLINA
RALEIGH ★
HICKORY •

★ COLUMBIA
SOUTH CAROLINA

ATLANTA

GEORGIA

ATLANTIC OCEAN

TALLAHASSEE

FLORIDA

Say the word beer, and one city comes to mind: yes, beloved old Milwaukee. But there's more to beer in the Midwest than Wisconsin's famous suds. The world's largest brewery, Anheuser-Busch, is on the border of Missouri and Illinois. And history buffs will enjoy visiting bars once frequented by John Dillinger, Eliot Ness, and other colorful characters.

MINNESOTA

August Schell Brewing Company (New Ulm). One of the oldest-surviving regional breweries in the U.S., dating back to 1860, and still operated by the same German-American family.

NEBRASKA

Upstream Brewing Company (Omaha). Located in the heart of Omaha's historic district, this brewpub is housed in a historically renovated, turn-of-the century firehouse.

KANSAS

The 75th Street Brewery (Kansas City). The city's first brewpub (founded in 1993) features beer varieties that are simply fun to order, including Cow Town Wheat and Possum Trot Brown Ale.

MISSOURI

COOL BREWERY TOUR: Anheuser-Busch (St. Louis). The world's biggest brewer. You may have heard of their pilsner, which they market under the name "Budweiser." (For more, see page 84.)

NORTH DAKOTA
★ BISMARCK

MINNESOTA

CHIPPEWA FA

SOUTH DAKOTA
★ PIERRE

ST. PAUL

NEW ULM

NEBRASKA
OMAHA
LINCOLN ★

IOV

DES MOINE

MISS

KANSAS
TOPEKA ★
JEFFERSON C

KAN

THE MIDWEST

WISCONSIN

The Jacob Leinenkugel Brewing Company (Chippewa Falls). The brewery, founded by Leinenkugel, a Bavarian immigrant, in 1867, offers a tour where you can see the original spring that Leinenkugel used to brew his beer and watch the wort as it makes its way through the brewing process.

NATIVE BEER: Milwaukee is the former home of Schlitz, Pabst, Jung, Husting, Graf, Milwaukee-Waukesha, and a host of forgotten breweries. Many originally settled here in the nineteenth century because of the abundant fresh water supply, as well as the quality of the grain available.

LAKE SUPERIOR

LAKE HURON

LAKE MICHIGAN

SCONSIN

MICHIGAN

ADISON ★

LANSING ★

WAUKEE •

DETROIT •

LAKE ERIE

• KALAMAZOO

CHICAGO •

• CLEVELAND

LINOIS

COLUMBUS ★

OHIO

INGFIELD ★

★ INDIANAPOLIS

INDIANA

• ST. LOUIS

MICHIGAN

Ye Old Tap Room (Detroit). The city's best beer bar, with an impressive selection of beers from around the world on hand at all times.

NATIVE BEER: Kalamazoo Brewing Company (Kalamazoo), makers of Bell's Beers and a great stout called Expedition.

OHIO

Great Lakes Brewing Co. Bar and Restaurant (Cleveland). The first Ohio microbrewery, it remains the best, producing popular brews such as Eliot Ness and Edmund Fitzgerald Porter—the first is named after the famous Untouchable; the second is named for a ship that sank in Lake Superior in 1975. Stick your fingers in the bullet holes in the walls, leftovers from the violent days of gangsters and Prohibition.

ILLINOIS

John Barleycorn (Chicago). John Dillinger once bought a round for the house with his ill-gotten gains. He was later shot and killed at the Biograph Theater, just two blocks away.

In the heat of the American Southwest, beer isn't a luxury—some days, it's damn near a necessity. But are you tough enough for one of Arizona's chili pepper beers? Or a visit to America's unofficial cheap beer capital in San Antonio, Texas?

ARIZONA

NATIVE BEER: Black Mountain Brewing Co. (Cave Creek) specializes in "chili beer." Each bottle of its trademark "Cave Creek Chili Beer" comes with a hand-picked chili pepper inside, delivering a hot, smoky, spicy punch with every sip. Yeeeeouch.

The Papago Brewing Company (Scottsdale). It brews 5 of its own beers, but also keeps 25 additional selections— many of them Southwest beers—on tap at all times, in addition to the 450 different domestic, foreign, and micro beers available for takeout.

The Rio Salado Brewing Company (Phoenix). It sounds like it might brew light, Corona-type pilsners, but it actually specializes in German ales, Märzens, and schwarzbiers. Brewmaster Tim Gossack runs a tour of the brewery every Saturday, a trip that ends up in the taproom for a mini sampling party.

DENVER
GOLDEN
COLORA
COLORADO RIVER
GRAND CANYON
ROCKY MOUNTAINS
SANTA FE
ARIZONA
PHOENIX
CAVE CREEK
SCOTTSDALE
NEW
MEXICO
RIO
GRANL

NEW MEXICO

The Santa Fe Brewing Company (Santa Fe). This maker of Sante Fe Pale Ale has used the same tabletop bottle capper (the "Super Colonna") on more than 1 million bottles of beer brewed since opening in 1992. The brewery record: 47 cases in 1 hour.

COLORADO

Wynkoop Brewing Company (Denver). Wynkoop hands out the "Beer Drinker of the Year Award" (see page 86) and brews Railyard Ale as well as Churchyard Ale.

Coors (Golden) is the country's fourth-largest brewery. Tours run every day except Sunday and holidays.

OKLAHOMA

Not an especially beer-friendly state, thanks to a law that says all beer must be under 3.2 percent alcohol by volume, which falls somewhere between near beer and Coors Light.

Coach's Restaurant and Brewery (Tulsa). The only real brewpub in these parts is a sports-type bar with sweet specials (90 cent happy hour) and delicious brews such as India pale ale and amber ale, despite the Oklahoma beer law. Coach's has two other locations, in Norman and Oklahoma City.

• TULSA

OKLAHOMA

OKLAHOMA CITY ★

DALLAS •

TEXAS

AUSTIN ★

SAN ANTONIO •

TEXAS

Adair's (Dallas). Famous for its beer, its live music, its half-pound burgers, and the bras that hang behind the bar for no apparent reason.

The Bitter End Bistro (Austin). The Bitter End is anything but—not with its lineup of Great American Beer Festival–winning ales and stouts, and the meals that fuse Southwest, Pacific Rim, Continental, and Caribbean fare.

People go on about Seattle and its coffee and grunge. But wake up and smell the beer, people—it's everywhere in the Pacific Northwest. If you want to see gorgeous, rolling fields of hops and barley, this is the place to go. The drinking is pretty good, too. From the burgeoning brewery scene in Portland to the sweet hopped mountains of the Golden State, the West is a beer lover's paradise.

OREGON

There are more breweries in Portland—20—than in any other city in the world. Yes, including cities in Belgium. Part of the reason might be that the Pacific Northwest is a huge hops-growing region, especially Oregon's Willamette Valley, the Yakima Valley in Washington, and the Snake River Valley in Idaho.

NATIVE BEERS: Where to begin? Portland favorites include beers from the Alameda Brewing Company, Full Sail Brewing Company, Hair of the Dog Brewing Company, BridgePort Brewing Company, and the Widmer Brothers Brewing Company. Rogue Ales, in Newport, was founded in 1988 by three former corporate executives. It makes some of the cheekiest beers around, including Dead Guy Ale, Shakespeare Stout, and Yellow Snow.

CALIFORNIA

Sierra Nevada (Chico). The biggest microbrewery in the U.S. offers a free tour to all ages, which means that there's no free beer at the end. But if you're of age, you can take advantage of a deal in the taproom, where you can sample two ounces (60 ml) of everything Sierra Nevada makes for eight bucks.

NATIVE BEER: The Anchor Brewing Company (San Francisco) single-handedly kicked off the microbrewery revolution (see page 26). You can thank founder Fritz Maytag for revitalizing "Steam Beer," a hybrid lager-ale that was originally popular during the California Gold Rush.

Heinold's Last Chance (Oakland), built from old whaling ship timber, is where tough-guy writer Jack London used to drink and story-swap.

WOODINV

SEATTLE
★ OLYMPIA
WASHINGTON

• PORTLAND
★ SALEM

OREGON

BO

CALIFORNIA

• CHICO

NEVAD

★ CARSON
★ SACRAMENTO

• SAN FRANCISCO
• OAKLAND

LAS VEGA

PACIFIC OCEAN

THE WEST

WASHINGTON

NATIVE BEER: Red Hook ESB (Woodinville), along with Samuel Adams and Sierra Nevada, became one of the most familiar microbrews during the 1990s. Back in the early 1980s, Red Hook's first offering—a spicy, Belgian-style ale—was mocked by some locals as "banana beer."

Big Time Brewing (Seattle) has been pouring its varieties of ale—many of them Great American Beer Festival winners—since 1988, a few years before Seattle became cool again.

MONTANA

Sip-N-Dip Lounge (Great Falls). The windows behind the bar look into the depths of the swimming pool at the O'Haire Motor Inn. The quality of the view depends, of course, on who's swimming and how much they work out.

WYOMING

NATIVE BEER: The Snake River Brewing Company (Jackson Hole) has racked up 15 gold and silver medals at the Great American Beer Festival since opening in an abandoned cinder block warehouse in 1994. Try the Pale Ale or Zonker Stout.

Lovejoy's Bar and Grill (Laramie) located in the heart of historic downtown Laramie, with a Union Pacific railroad line right across the street. The half-pound burgers are pretty good, too.

UTAH

State law says that no beer can be stronger than .2 percent alcohol by weight. Since most of the country measures alcohol by volume, it's not as bad as it sounds—it comes out to about 4 percent ABV. Still, a six-pack of Utah beer will only get you as drunk as a five-pack elsewhere.

The Red Rock Brewing Company (Salt Lake City). Tasty beer styles—Bavarian weiss, Irish ale, Vienna Lager, Dunkel Weizen—belie the Utah beer laws.

Oh, Canada. Beer drinkers from the Great White North were honored (?) in the 1983 comedy *Strange Brew* (see page 182). The first Canadian beer was believed to be a weird spruce-needle beer concocted by the native inhabitants who lived near Quebec in 1535. It was high in vitamin C, but, unfortunately, tasted like tree bark. In 1919, Canada decided to enact a nation-wide prohibition of alcohol . . . but, uh, well, changed its mind two years later. This meant that a lot of Canadian brewers made a killing sneaking their beer and spirits down to the U.S., which is why Eliot Ness (Kevin Costner) was perched at the U.S./Canadian border in the 1987 Brian DePalma movie *The Untouchables*.

YUKON   NORTHWEST TERRITORIES

NUNA

BRITISH COLUMBIA

The Longwood Brewpub (Nanaimo) offers a Saturday afternoon tour led by brewer Harley Smith. If you're 19 or older, you can sample four of Smith's beers—for instance, the Longwood Ale, Dunkelwiezenbrau, Two-Penny Ale, or Copper Bock—in 6-oz. (175 ml) "taster" glasses at tour's end.

BRITISH COLUMBIA

MANITOB

ALBERTA

SASKATCHEW

ROCKY MOUNTAINS

SASKATOON •

CALGARY

PACIFIC OCEAN

NANAIMO •

ALBERTA

Limerick's Traditional Public House (Calgary) is a two-floor, Celtic-style pub offering a rotating stock of 45 draught beers from around the world—with a keen eye toward the Emerald Isle, of course—and, if the mood strikes you, 25 different single malt scotches.

SASKATCHEWAN

Athena Restaurant & Specklebelly's Brew Pub (Saskatoon). Okay, I admit it—I included this relaxed pub with an excellent bar menu because of the name. Would someone named "Specklebelly" ever lead you astray?

MANITOBA

Fort Garry Brewing Company (Winnipe is an old-time brewery dating back to t 1920s; like so many other small brewer in the post–WWII era, it was sold to a giant brewer (in this case, Molson). Fortunately, brewer Richard D. Hoesche resurrected Fort Garry 34 years later an started producing his signature dark al and pale ales.

AVERAGE ANNUAL BEER CONSUMPTION IN LITERS

Canada 71

| 0 | 25 | 50 | 75 | 100 | 125 | 150 |

CANADA

NEWFOUNDLAND

NOVA SCOTIA

QUEBEC

ATLANTIC OCEAN

PRINCE EDWARD ISLAND

NEW BRUNSWICK

ONTARIO

NNIPEG

CHAMBLY•
MONTREAL • ⓐ
OTTAWA ★

ⓑ• SAINT JOHN

GREAT LAKES TORONTO • ⓒ

NEW BRUNSWICK

NATIVE BEER: Moosehead Breweries Ltd. (Saint John) is headquartered here. Remember when Moosehead was all the rage in the '80s?

QUEBEC

NATIVE BEER: Unibroue (Chambly), one of Canada's most successful microbreweries, was founded by a famous Canadian rock singer, Robert Charlebois. Try the Blanche de Chambly, a Belgian wheat beer. If you're adventurous, try the Quelque Chose, a spiced cherry beer.

NATIVE BEER: Molson (Montreal) was founded in 1786 on the banks of the St. Lawrence River, making it the oldest beer brand in North America. Useless fact: Later, founder John Molson created the first all-Canadian-made steamboat.

ONTARIO

NATIVE BEER: The Labatt Brewing Company (Toronto) was born in 1847 when John Kinder Labatt arrived in London, Ontario. He wrote to his wife, "I have been considering this brewing affair for some time, and I think it would suit me better than anything else."

According to the history books, Mexican beer can trace its tradition way back to . . . the Czech Republic? It's true. In the sixteenth century, the Emperor of Vienna sent a Czech brewmaster to Mexico to teach the residents how to make a proper beer, and Mexicans have been enjoying it ever since. (Mexico's modern-day Bohemia beer is named after this generous contribution.) Even though Mexico's most famous export beer (Corona) demands a wedge of lime, you don't have to add fruit to enjoy the wide variety of south-of-the-border brews.

TECATE

CIUDAD ACUNA

SIERRA MADRE OCCIDENTAL

GULF OF CALIFORNIA

MEXICO

The Tecate Brewery Tour (Tecate), about 40 miles east of Tijuana, is a feature of many Baja travel packages, but I suggest you skip the other nonsense and head straight for the brewery. After your 90-minute Saturday morning tour, you can sit in an open-air beer garden and enjoy free samples.

Señor Frog's (Mazatlán). Now a giant chain with locations in Spain, Brazil, and the United States, this popular restaurant began here in 1971. The food is cheap, the beer is plentiful, and the sight of tourists dressed in foam frog hats is unforgettable.

MAZATLÁ

PUERTO VALLARTA

Yelapa (Puerto Vallarta). If you'd prefer to avoid the tourist traps, try this local favorite in the Plaza Las Glorias Hotel. Raise a glass as you listen to live Mariachi and Marimba music.

PACIFIC OCEAN

NATIVE BEER: Grupo Modelo (Mexico City), makers of Corona, Leon, Modelo Especial, Negra Modelo, Pacifico, and Victoria. (For more, see page 91.)

The Dubliner (Mexico City). Absolutely need a pint of Guinness while you're south of the border? You're in luck—a minor Irish pub craze has swept Mexico City in recent years.

LEGAL DRINKING AGE: 18

NUMBER OF BREWERIES: 5

HOW TO SAY "CHEERS": "Salud!"
(pronounced sah-LOOD)

NATIVE BEERS: Tecate (a), Dos Equis
(b), Sol (c), Corona (d), Modelo
Especial (e), Negra Modelo (f)

The Corona Club (Ciudad Acuna) was featured
in the 1995 Robert Rodriguez shoot-'em-up,
Desperado. (For more, see page 189.)

NATIVE BEER: Especialidades Cerveceras (Apodaca), makers of Casta (Spanish for "purity") Beers, including Bruna (a
pale ale) and Triguera (a wheat beer).

Cervecería Cuauhtémoc Moctezuma (Monterrey), makers
of Tecate, Tecate Light, Carta Blanca, Superior, Sol, Dos
Equis, Indio, Bohemia, and Noche Buena—a south-of-the-
border Christmas lager. The brewery is located in the heart
of the city and the tour is surprisingly detailed—expect to
spend at least two hours there. Some visitors opt to linger
in the beer garden all day long.

APODOCA
MONTERREY
©

RRA MADRE
RIENTAL

GULF OF
MEXICO

ⓓ ⓔ ⓕ

★ MEXICO CITY

COOL FACT: If you find yourself in Mexico between December 1
and January 1, be sure to snag a bottle of Noche Buena—a dark
Christmas lager that people rave about. It's not exported, and not
available any other time of the year.

AVERAGE ANNUAL BEER CONSUMPTION IN LITERS

Mexico 48						
0	25	50	75	100	125	150

THE CARIBBEAN

Most people associate the Caribbean with fruit-flavored rum drinks, but there's plenty here for beer drinkers, too. Languages, drinking ages, and native beers will vary from island to island, but one thing is certain: Virtually any beer tastes halfway decent when you're drinking it on a sandy beach under a clear sky.

CUBA

NATIVE BEERS: Hatuey Beer (named for the Indian chief whose face graces its label) is readily available all over Miami. It's a tradition to share this beer with a friend—ask a Cuban bartender for "un indio y dos canoas" ("an Indian and two canoes"), and he'll give you a cold bottle of Hatuey and two small glasses.

BAHAMAS

Shenanigan's Irish Pub (Freeport). An Irish pub? In the Bahamas? I don't make this stuff up, folks. Shenanigan's serves a host of Irish beers, shepherd's pie, even bangers and mash.

• FREEPORT

• HAVANA

CAYMAN ISLANDS

NATIVE BEERS: Stingray Premium. Enjoy one on behalf of your offshore accounts.

• NEGRIL BEACH

HAITI
SANTO DOMINGO •

JAMAICA

Rick's Café (Negril Beach). This cliff-top bar offers beautiful sunsets, endless bottles of Red Stripe, and (I kid you not) amateur cliff diving. Don't drink and dive.

ARUBA

NATIVE BEERS: Crack open a Balashi, a golden-colored pilsner with a well-balanced aftertaste.

ANTILLES

DOMINICAN REPUBLIC

NATIVE BEERS: The Dominican Republic is the sixth-largest exporter of beer to the United States, thanks to the success of local favorite Presidente. If you don't have your passport up to date, look for Presidente in Florida and northern New Jersey. It's showing up in other parts of the world, too.

PUERTO RICO

Hotel Milano (Old San Juan). In the heart of the old city. Take the elevator all the way up and enjoy the view from the Panorama Bar, a rooftop beer garden.

VIRGIN ISLANDS (U.S.)

NATIVE BEERS: Try Blackbeard Ale and Foxy's Lager, both brewed by the Virgin Islands Brewing Company on the St. Croix waterfront.

ANTIGUA

NATIVE BEERS: Wadadli is practically synonymous with "beer" in Antigua. Its name derives from the native people's original name for their island.

AN JUAN

ONTSERRAT
UADELOUPE
DOMINICA
MARTINIQUE
SAINT VINCENT

GRENADA

SAINT LUCIA

NATIVE BEERS: Ti-Malt is brewed by The Windward & Leeward Brewery in Vieux Fort. The taste is maltier than most other beers, and has a surprising hint of toffee.

BARBADOS

Pay a visit to the Banks Brewery, which makes such local favorites as Banks Beer, Tiger Malt, and XXTRA Strong Brew. They even have a "Beer Gear" store if you want to shop for accessories.

TRINIDAD AND TOBAGO

NATIVE BEERS: Try the national beer, Carib Lager, or its close cousins, Carib Shandy and Royal Extra Stout.

CHINA AND JAPAN

CHINA

Chinese beer has come a long way since *samshu*, a simple beer made from wheat that dates back to ancient times. These days, despite a relatively low annual beer consumption, China is poised to overtake the U.S. as the largest beer market in the world, thanks to its enormous population. Over the past 20 years, beer has slowly emerged as the number one alcoholic beverage here, and it's especially popular in major cities. The world's biggest brewers are vying for market dominance, but many Chinese drinkers remain faithful to the national brew, Tsingtao. The upcoming China beer wars will be interesting to watch.

LEGAL DRINKING AGE: **18 to pur-chase, 21 to drink on the premises**

NUMBER OF BREWERIES: **600**

HOW TO SAY "CHEERS": **"Yung sing"**

NATIVE BEERS: **Yanjing (a), Beijing (b) Tsingtao (c), Reeb (d), Huiquan (e)**

GOBI DESERT

CHINA

GREAT W CH

NATIVE BEERS: Tsingtao (Qingdao), pronounced "ching-dow," is probably the Asian beer most Westerners are familiar with, only because it seems to be stocked at most Chinese restaurants. It was first brewed in 1903 by German settlers who came to Qingdoa and apparently realized there wasn't much in the way of decent beer around. Tsingtao also happens to be China's biggest export.

Long Bar (Shanghai) features, well, a really loooonnnnnng bar that spans the entire length of the joint. Oddly enough, it is a favorite of sports fans as well as Chinese fashionistas—fashion shows are held here regularly.

NATIVE BEER: Reeb (Shanghai). Tsingtao may dominate in the rest of the country, but Reeb, produced by the Shanghai Mila Brewery Company, is the most popular beer in this area, and accounts for one out of every three beers consumed here.

AVERAGE ANNUAL BEER CONSUMPTION IN LITERS

China 16						
Japan 56.4						
0	25	50	75	100	125	150

JAPAN

Beer was introduced to Japan during the middle of the nineteenth century, and since then it's been giving sake (technically a type of rice beer) a run for its money—Japan is the fifth-largest consumer of beer in the world in terms of sheer volume. The first batch of Japanese beer was brewed in 1853 by a doctor named Koumin Kawamoto, who followed a recipe in a Dutch book. Today, Japanese beers are renowned for their clean, ultracrisp taste and unique, oversized containers.

LEGAL DRINKING AGE: 18 to purchase, 21 to drink on the premises

NUMBER OF BREWERIES: 33

HOW TO SAY "CHEERS": "Kampai" (pronounced kam-pie)

NATIVE BEERS: Sapporo Draft (f), Asahi Draft (g), Kirin Lager (h), Suntory (i)

SAPPORO • (f)

JAPAN

EAST CHINA SEA

BEIJING

QUINGDAO (g) SUITA •
(c) OSAKA •

TOKYO ★ (h)
SHIBUYA •
(i)

(d)
SHANGHAI

(e) • HUIAN

NATIVE BEERS: The two most popular are Sapporo (based in, you guessed it, Sapporo), which is popular in the U.S. for its oversized, sculpted-steel can that could double as a deadly weapon, and Asahi (Suita), which was founded in 1892 and the following year won a prize at the World's Fair in Chicago. It would take almost 100 years, though, for Asahi to be available in the U.S.

Billy Barew's Beer Bar (Tokyo). It sounds American, but features 120 different brews from around the world. Can't make up your mind? The staff is known for making smart beer suggestions for you.

Belgo (Shibuya). It's literally a supermarket of beer. You pick out what you want from the refrigerated coolers, then bring it to the counter and pay for it. But unlike most supermarkets, you can sit down at Belgo and enjoy your beer right there.

NATIVE BEERS: Suntory Beer (Osaka) entered the Japanese market in 1963, claiming to be the pioneer of Japanese draft beer. Surprisingly, their biggest seller is a malt liquor called Suntory Malts.

AUSTRALIA

Predictably, beer was on board when England's Captain Cook first made his way to Australia on the *Endeavor* in 1768. He had four tons of beer on board, and his crew drank it all just one month into the voyage. Clearly, Australia needed to get busy making its own beer. These days, the country offers an amazing variety of beers—and an amazingly inconsistent range of serving sizes. In Western Australia, ask for a schooner (15 ounces [440 ml]) or a pot (20 ounces [590 ml]). In South Australia, ask for a pint (15 ounces [440 ml]) or a schooner (10 ounces [295 ml]). In Queensland, ask for a pot (10 ounces [295 ml]) or a jug (40 ounces [1.2 l]). If you think it's confusing now, wait until you've tossed back a few.

LEGAL DRINKING AGE: 18 to purchase, 21 to drink on premises

NUMBER OF BREWERIES: 85

HOW TO SAY "CHEERS": "Kia ora" (pronounced kee AH orr AH)

NATIVE BEERS: Emu (a), Dogbolter (b), Coopers (c), Thirsty Dog (d), Foster's (e), Tooheys (f), Victoria Bitter (g), Cascade (h)

NORTHE
TERRITO

AUSTRAL

WESTERN
AUSTRALIA

XXXX Brewery (Brisbane). Known as "barbed wire" among Queenslanders (because that's what the name looks like), XXXX offers a 45-minute walking tour of its brewery—and occasional nighttime barbecues!

SOUTH
AUSTRAL

PERTH
FREMANTLE • • CANNING-VALE

NATIVE BEER: Sail & Anchor (Fremantle). This popular brewery—a regular winner in the Australian International Beer Awards—features interactive tours seven days a week. The cover charge includes tastings of six different hand-crafted beers.

Swan Brewery (Canning Vale). The largest brewery in Western Australia, with a history that dates back to 1837. Call in advance to arrange a tour, and be sure to sample the Emu while you're there.

NATIVE BEER: Piss (Melbourne). That's not a misprint or a tourist prank. It's actually a low-calorie, all-natural beer—in other words, the Australian version of lite beer.

AVERAGE ANNUAL BEER CONSUMPTION IN LITERS

	0	25	50	75	100	125	150
Australia 84							
New Zealand 84							

NEW ZEALAND

The Other Land Down Under has a thriving beer-brewing industry, as well as a national beer competition called the New Zealand Beer Cup (recently merged with the New Zealand International Beer Awards). Steinlager is one of the most popular exports, but quirky local favorites abound.

LEGAL DRINKING AGE: 18 to purchase, 21 to drink on the premises

NUMBER OF BREWERIES: 16

HOW TO SAY "CHEERS": "Kia ora," (pronounced kee AH orr AH)

NATIVE BEERS: Steinlager (i), Tui Ale (j), Bays Gold Lager (k)

COOL FACT: New Zealand was the first country in the world to introduce the eight-hour workday. (Which, of course, leaves more time to drink beer after work. Cheers to NZ!)

GREAT BARRIER REEF

NATIVE BEER: Australis (Auckland). As if all the different serving sizes in Australia weren't confusing enough, Australis beer is actually brewed in New Zealand.

EENSLAND

DARLING RIVER (d)

• BRISBANE

NEW ZEALAND

V SOUTH
ALES (e)(f)

SYDNEY •

NCY PARK

CANBERRA ★

ICTORIA

(g) • MELBOURNE

TASMAN
SEA

NORTH ISLAND

BAY OF PLENTY

(i)

• AUCKLAND

(j)

• MANGATAINOKA
WELLINGTON ★

(k)

TAHUNANUI •

TASMANIA

• HOBART

(h)

SOUTH ISLAND

SOUTHERN ALPS

• RENWICK

• DUNEDIN

NATIVE BEER: McDuff's (Dunedin). This was originally called "Duff Beer," but a legal threat from the producers of *The Simpsons* forced brewery owner Gavin Duff to add a "Mc" to its name.

NATIVE BEER: Pink Elephant (Renwick). It's not named after the mythical creatures you might see if you drink too much beer. The creator's name is Roger Pink, and he's always had a thing for elephants.

BEER CONNOISSEURSHIP

"It is my aim to win the American people over to our side, to make them all lovers of beer."—*Adolphus Busch*

You can pop the top and drain it quickly. You can pour it into a plastic funnel. You can carefully and lovingly decant it into a crystal goblet. You can clink mugs of it together with your best friend. But whatever you do, you should know how to appreciate and respect your beer. In this section, we will dive deep into the things that make a beer great, flavorful, cold, cheap, or whatever it is you enjoy about it.

A FIELD GUIDE TO BEER

You've probably heard there are two types of beer: good beer and bad beer. Bad beer, when offered free of charge, can magically become good beer. But you could also say that there are two other types of beer: blue-collar beer and fancy-pants beer. Or is it cheap beer and expensive beer? Or warm beer and ice-cold beer? Good beer and American beer?

In fact, there really are two types of beer: lagers and ales. But before we get to those, let's take a moment to honor the ingredients in almost every glass of beer.

THE INGREDIENTS

WATER

Many breweries make a big deal about their water. Coors is brewed from "fresh Colorado springs," while Bass is made with Burton water, which is "famous for its purity." But water does make a big difference. Beer is more than 90 percent water, after all, and different kinds of water (soft, brackish, chlorinated, etc.) react differently with various ingredients. Early breweries used to choose their locations based on fresh and constant water supplies.

GRAINS

The basic building block of any beer. Without grains, yeast would have nothing to ferment, and your beer would have no color—no golden hues, no dark, luscious finish. The darker the grains, the darker the beer. Malted grains also tend to be sweet, a result counterbalanced by the bitter taste of hops (see next ingredient). Barley is the usual suspect in many beers, though some brewers use wheat or rye to change the taste a bit. Some popular American beers add corn or rice to the mix to lighten the beer, and to keep costs down.

HOPS

Hops are plants, and they're actually part of the same botanical family as hemp. In A.D. 1200, beer-brewing monks first discovered that hops both preserve beer and give it that distinctive, slightly bitter taste. The higher-quality microbrews spend a lot of time picking and choosing the best kinds of hop varieties; some even brag about using the whole hop cone, as opposed to extracts or pellets of hops.

FLAVORS (OPTIONAL)

Back in the days when beer was a little on the rough side, it was common practice to add other flavors to smooth things out. This is why the ancient Egyptians laced their beer with fruits and berries. Today, brewers will add flavors just for fun, such as coriander seeds, chocolate, coffee, peaches, clover, chiles, cinnamon, and cherries.

YEAST

This is where the magic happens. Yeast is a type of fungus that can travel through the air and has the amazing ability to turn sugar into alcohol. Yeast is also a hearty microorganism; some breweries have been using the same strains of yeast for hundreds of years. Yeast also plays a critical role in determining whether a beer becomes an ale or a lager. Read on.

Hopped up on something: A field of luscious green hops, along with barley (inset), and three roasts—light, medium, and dark.

ALE

Ale was the first kind of beer ever brewed. Ale is "top fermented," which means that the yeast hangs out on top of the tank, working its magic in warm temperatures. Warm, top-fermenting yeast has a much faster turnaround time; the result can be a fruitier, heavier, earthier, more complex beer. Some varieties include:

BITTER/EXTRA SPECIAL/EXTRA BITTER (ESB)

These ale styles are high in hops and malt, and low in carbonation; the ESB has more of an alcohol kick. Try Boddington's Pub Ale, Fuller's ESB, or Redhook ESB.

INDIA PALE ALE (IPA)

This ale was brewed by the English specifically for its citizens in India—the beer had to be high in alcohol and hops to survive the long voyage. If you're a little unclear about what hops taste like, order an IPA—these are pretty much the hoppiest beers you can get. Try Victory HopDevil IPA or Harpoon IPA.

LAMBIC

Lambics take the idea of top fermentation one step further. Whereas other beers are covered to prevent exposure to wild airborne yeasts, brewers leave lambics in an open container, allowing foreign yeasts to settle in and wreak havoc. The result is typically a very daring beer. Try Boon Gueuze or Lindemans Framboise.

PALE ALE

As the name implies, these ales are lighter; they're brewed with a lighter roasted malt, but still have a decent hops factor. Try Sierra Nevada Pale Ale, Bass Pale Ale, Anchor Liberty Ale, Sam Adams Boston Ale, or Saranac Pale Ale.

PORTER

A dark beer that pretty much went extinct until adventurous microbrewers resurrected the style. If you enjoy your brew with a big hunk of dark chocolate, porter's the beer to order. Try Yuengling Porter or Sierra Nevada Porter.

STOUT

The darkest beer going, infused with coffee and chocolate flavors, and with a body fuller than John Goodman at a funnel cake stand. Try Guinness Stout, Murphy's Irish Stout, Beamish Irish Stout, Samuel Smith Oatmeal Stout, or Shakespeare Stout.

WHEAT BEERS

Some brewers will use wheat in place of—or in addition to—barley. The result is a beer that's slightly cloudy, tart, and highly carbonated. Wheat beers also tend to have fewer calories and carbohydrates. Try Schneider Weisse, Pyramid Hefeweizen, or Sierra Nevada Wheat Beer.

LAGER

Lager (rhymes with "frogger") is probably the type of beer you first chugged in high school. Lagers are bottom-fermented, which means the yeast works at the bottom of the vat, resulting in a cleaner, smoother beer. Years ago, brewers would have to cease production of their ales in summer, because the air was too full of wild yeasts. Brewers in Bavaria discovered that cold air would control the yeast and started to make the first primitive lagers in the Alps. (*Lager* is a German word that means "to store.") It wasn't until the 1860s that brewers started to study yeasts under a microscope, and could scientifically pinpoint the exact temperatures needed to brew smooth lager. Today, most of the beer consumed in the world—especially at your local sports bar—is a type of lager. Varieties include . . .

PILSNER

The term applies to any workaday lager, but purists reserve it for beers styled after the originals brewed in Pilsen, in the Czech Republic. Golden, malty, and slightly bitter, pilsners have divided and taken over the beer world. You're probably familiar with Bud and Miller, so try Pilsner Urquell, Budweiser Budvar, Victory's Prima Pils, or Brooklyn Pilsner.

BOCK

Bock is German for "strong beer," and that's a nice description. Bocks are darker, stronger, and aged longer than most lagers. Bocks used to be brewed late in the harvest season, stored all winter long, and tapped at the end of winter or on the first warm day of spring. A stronger version is known as doppelbock. Try Aass Bock, Shiner Bavarian Bock, or St. Nick Bock.

MÄRZEN/OKTOBERFEST

Märzens are the opposite of bocks—in terms of season, anyway. They are brewed in the spring to be consumed the following fall, and are made hearty and full of malt to last through the hot summer. Try Great Lakes Eliot Ness, Paulaner Oktoberfest Märzen Amber, Samuel Adams Octoberfest, or Spaten Oktoberfest Ur-Märzen.

SCHWARZBIER

The lager version of porter—dark, dark stuff. Try Köstritzer Schwarzbier or Saranac Black Forest.

MALT LIQUOR

Basically, these are stronger, sweeter versions of ordinary lager. According to some state laws, any beer that's more than 5 percent alcohol is deemed a "malt liquor." Drinking malt liquor is not about the journey, it's about the destination. Try (if you dare) Colt 45, Mickey's, St. Ides, or Schlitz Malt Liquor Bull.

The Weirdest Beer Flavors on Earth

For hundreds of years, brewers have experimented with various flavors to enhance their beers. Sometimes this gets out of hand. Here's a short list of some of the strangest-sounding beers I've seen, but simply can't bring myself to drink.

Vanilla Cream Stout (Lawson Creek Brewery)

Crazy Ed's Cave Creek Chili Beer (Black Mountain Brewing Company)

Chocolate Raspberry Stout (Anacapa Brewing Company)

White Chocolate Mousse (Dixie Brewing Company)

Longshot Hazelnut Ale (Boston Beer Company)

St. Peter's Lemon and Ginger Spiced Ale (St. Peter's Brewing Company)

Banana Lambic (Chappeau)

Hemp Ale (Sioux Falls Brewing Company)

THE BIG BEERS

In 1965, the top five brewers in the U.S. were Anheuser-Busch, Schlitz, Pabst, Falstaff, and Carling. Forty years later, the list is quite different—only Anheuser-Busch is still in the business of brewing beer. It's not just a case of breweries folding, either; in the 1990s brewers merged like drunken college freshmen. As of this printing (2004), here are some of the biggest brewers in the world, producing the most gallons of beer per year. Let's hoist one to the big guys, okay?

ANHEUSER-BUSCH
ST. LOUIS, MISSOURI

ON TAP: BUDWEISER, BUD LIGHT, MICHELOB, MICHELOB ULTRA, MICHELOB AMBERBOCK, BUSCH, NATURAL LIGHT, BACARDI SILVER, O'DOUL'S

Truly, the King of Beers. Anheuser-Busch has dominated the market for the past 60 years, and there's no slowing it down. One out of every five beers sipped in the United States is a Bud. The brewery was created by Adolphus Busch, who was born the second-youngest of 22(!) children in 1839 in Kastel, Germany, and immigrated to the U.S. in 1857. Originally, Adolphus worked for a commission house in 1859 in St. Louis. He and a friend then started their own brewery supply company. Busch founded his own brewing supply businesses; by 1861 he was married to Lilly, the daughter of one of Busch's clients, Eberhard Anheuser. Busch bought out Anheuser's partner eight years later, and by 1876, he introduced Budweiser.

Bud became the first national beer, and it would come to rule the planet. Seriously. If you can find a sports bar or neighborhood tavern between the Pacific and Atlantic Oceans that doesn't sell Budweiser, I'll send you a crisp fiver.

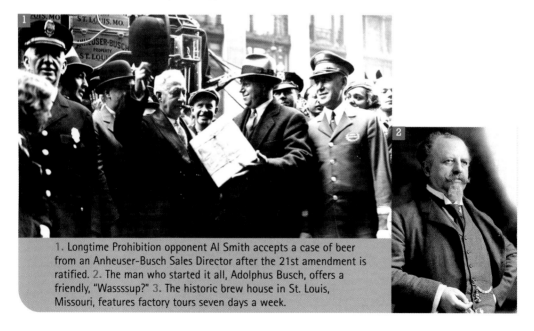

1. Longtime Prohibition opponent Al Smith accepts a case of beer from an Anheuser-Busch Sales Director after the 21st amendment is ratified. 2. The man who started it all, Adolphus Busch, offers a friendly, "Wassssup?" 3. The historic brew house in St. Louis, Missouri, features factory tours seven days a week.

(Above) Site of the world's very first "Miller Time." (At right) The man behind the beer, Frederick Edward John Miller.

SAB-MILLER
MILWAUKEE, WISCONSIN
ON TAP: MILLER HIGH LIFE, MILLER LITE, MILLER GENUINE DRAFT, MEISTER BRAU, MILWAUKEE'S BEST, RED DOG, OLD ENGLISH 800, MICKEY'S, MAGNUM 40, ICEHOUSE, SOUTHPAW LIGHT, SHARP'S

Thanks to a June 2002 merger of South African Breweries (SAB) and Miller Brewing, the new SAB-Miller instantly became the second-largest beer maker in the world. Miller was founded by Frederick Edward John Miller, a tall, spare man who was the scion of wealthy German politicians, and who learned the beer business under the tutelage of his brewer uncle. By 1854, Miller and his young family had crossed the Atlantic and settled in Milwaukee, proclaiming that "a town with a magnificent harbor like that has a great future in store." Miller purchased the five-year-old Plank Road Brewery for $8,000, renamed it the Fred Miller Brewing Company, and got to work. (Years later, Miller would introduce fancier beers under the "Plank Road Brewery" label.)

Miller's beer was immediately successful among Milwaukee residents, especially the recent German émigrés, many of whom enjoyed weekends at the Miller Beer Garden, established shortly after Miller took over the plant. Three generations of Millers turned the brewery into a national beer powerhouse, and in 1969, Philip Morris purchased the highly profitable company. Today, Miller not only brews its own formidable line of beers, but also contracts more beer than you can shake a stick at—including all of the old-style beers formerly brewed by Pabst. This is slightly ironic because the Plank Road Brewery was originally owned by Charles Best, the son of Pabst founder Philip Best.

HEINEKEN BROUWERIJEN B.V.
AMSTERDAM, NETHERLANDS
ON TAP: HEINEKEN, AMSTEL, VOS, TIGER

On December 16, 1863, a 22-year-old Dutchman named Gerard Adriaan Heineken purchased a 300-year-old brewery in Amsterdam and started brewing a newfangled bottom-fermenting beer called "lager." Soon, the brewery surpassed national competitors such as Oranjeboom and Amstel and started thinking internationally. Today, Heineken is probably the best-known export beer in the United States, and that's not by accident. A mere three days after Prohibition ended, Heineken was already unloading barrels of beer in Hoboken, New Jersey, eager to slake the thirst of Americans. In 1940, Nazi occupation of the Netherlands put the kibosh on exports of beer; it wasn't until May 1945—when the German army surrendered—that Heineken was free to seek American shores again. By 1947, an emboldened Heineken would proclaim that its beer was "more superior to all American beers." In 1968, Heineken took over its major Dutch competitor, Amstel, and later, riding the "light" craze, introduced Amstel Light, which actually surpassed Heineken as the best-selling export beer in the United States. Today Heineken is the largest brewer in Europe, and the third-largest brewery in the world.

Imagine Willy Wonka Wonka's chocolate factory—with free beer. That's what the Heineken brewery tour is like.

INTERBREW
BRUSSELS, BELGIUM

ON TAP: STELLA ARTOIS, BECK'S, BASS ALE, LABATT'S, BODDINGTONS, BOHEMIA, DOS EQUIS, HOEGAARDEN, LABATT'S, LEFFE, ORANJEBOOM, ST. PAULI GIRL, ROLLING ROCK, MANY OTHER REGIONAL BRANDS

It's tempting to compare Interbrew, the fourth-largest brewer in the world, to the Borg from *Star Trek: The Next Generation*. It's an ancient group that travels the beer universe, assimilating as many regional breweries as it can, so that the strength of the individual can be transferred to the collective. Its flagship brews around the world are Stella Artois and Beck's, but its marketing strategy says it all: "Our main marketing objectives are to promote a domestic lager brand to be our primary brand in each market, to support this primary brand with at least one other brand in our portfolio, and to enhance Stella Artois' status as an international brand." It's not poetry, but the plan is working: Interbrew beers are either brewed, licensed, or sold in most of the world, except for parts of the Middle East, Africa, and South America.

Interbrew started out way back in 1366 as a brewery called Den Hoorn. In 1717, it evolved into Artois, the makers of Stella Artois. Then in the 1990s, the company became merger-crazy, scooping up Labatt in Canada, Bass Brewers in Britain, Beck & Co in Germany, Rolling Rock in the United States, SUN Interbrew in Russia, and countless others. In short, if you've got a beer in your hand, there's a strong chance it's either from Bud, Miller, Heineken, or Interbrew. Resistance is futile.

The building below bears a striking resemblance to the Borg "cube."

1. Carlsberg's historic Dipylon gate, built in 1892. 2. Professor Emil Christian Hansen, the Carlsberg wizard who discovered pure yeast. 3. Carl Jacobson, son of founder J. C. Jacobsen.

CARLSBERG BREWERIES A/S
COPENHAGEN, DENMARK

ON TAP: CARLSBERG, DOUBLE DIAMOND, ELEPHANT RED, TETLEY'S ENGLISH ALE, TUBORG

On November 10, 1847, the first Carlsberg beer was created, and a European empire was born. The brewery was founded by J. C. Jacobsen, who is remembered for his various beer innovations, including the 1883 development of a strain of pure yeast known as *Saccharomyces carlsbergensis*. With the advent of pure yeast, a brewer could ensure that his beer would always taste the same, whether it was brewed in 1883 or 1913. Jacobsen's son formed his own brewery, which eventually merged with his old man's company. By the early 1930s, more than half of the beer exported to Great Britain was Carlsberg beer. Various luminaries paid their respects to Carlsberg, including Winston Churchill, who visited in 1950; Queen Elizabeth II, who visited the same year; and Orson Welles, who gave voice to the company's famous slogan, "Probably the best lager in the world." Today, Carlsberg sells more than 7.9 billion liters of beer per year.

NEWCASTLE BREWERIES LTD.
NEWCASTLE UPON TYNE, UNITED KINGDOM
ON TAP: NEWCASTLE BROWN ALE

Newcastle Brown Ale is a spunky beer, produced by even spunkier brewers. When an Australian company made a hostile-takeover bid in 1988, Newcastle started shipping bottles with the label upside-down as part of a "Keep Us on Top" public-relations campaign. The plan worked; the Aussies were repelled. Historians think that Newcastle, England, was the first place in the country where beer was brewed; Newcastle Breweries, Ltd., was formed in 1890 after merging several smaller breweries in the area. By the 1930s, Newcastle's trademark Brown Ale (or as it pronounced it then, "Broon Ale") was a huge hit in the town of North East, England, especially among the working class. When Newcastle merged with Scottish Brewers in 1960, Brown Ale started to swim to distant shores, but still remained wildly popular on the home front. The phrase "I'm going to walk the dog" soon became a North East expression for "I'm off to the pub for a bottle of Newcastle," and ads in the 1980s featured cans opening to the sound of "Woof!" By the 1990s, Newcastle ruled England, and became the best-selling bottled beer in Europe.

1. Hauling Brown Ale along the Tyne River. 2. Packing cases at the original Newcastle Brewery.

An evening view of Mexico's megabrewery.

GRUPO MODELO/CERVECERIA MODELO/CORONA
MEXICO CITY, MEXICO

ON TAP: CORONA, LEON, MODELO ESPECIAL, NEGRA MODELO, PACIFICO, VICTORIA

Grupo Modelo is the Budweiser of Mexico, and its best-known beer, Corona, is a favorite of anyone who's ever shoved a wedge of lime down its neck. Grupo Modelo was founded in October 1925; before then, Mexican beer lovers depended on small, regional breweries to satisfy their thirst. Grupo Modelo was different. It wanted to be the nation's leading brewery, and soon became just that through acquisitions, mergers, and some pretty damned fine beers. Grupo Modelo's patron saint is Don Pablo Diez Fernandez, an extremely shrewd businessman who joined the company soon after it started and helped make Corona a hugely successful export beer.

KIRIN BREWERY COMPANY, LIMITED
TOKYO, JAPAN

ON TAP: KIRIN ICHIBAN, KIRIN LAGER, KIRIN LIGHT

According to legend, the Kirin—a mystical half dragon—once encountered a beautiful woman and "enveloped her in his sacred breath." (Apparently, that's a Japanese euphemism for the horizontal mambo.) A year later, that beautiful woman gave birth to Confucius, a vast source of wisdom and fortune cookie messages. Believe in the Kirin or don't, but there's no denying the father of Kirin beer was also a strange hybrid: an American brewer, William Copeland, who set up shop in Japan in 1869. The next year, the Spring Valley Brewery was born in a Tokyo suburb. By 1884, it had failed. British and German businessmen bought the remnants and launched the Japan Brewery

Company, Ltd. Three years later, it introduced a German-style lager called Kirin, named after the mythical beast. Confucius didn't have to be around to label it a hit. Kirin first made its way to North America in 1987, with the help of Molson Canada. Today, it accounts for 40 percent of the beer sold in Japan and is the fourth-largest export worldwide.

"Okay, fellas—smile and say 'Smokey and the Bandit!'"

COORS BREWING COMPANY
GOLDEN, COLORADO

ON TAP: COORS, KEYSTONE, KILLIAN'S, BLUE MOON

Is there a Coors family curse? The brewery's founder, Adolph Coors, died in a freak accident in 1929, when he was stricken with the flu and accidentally fell out of a sixth-floor hotel room. Coors's son, Adolph Jr., was abducted and murdered by a man who would make the FBI's Ten Most Wanted List. Not good. Fortunately, the beer has had the opposite luck. Founded in 1873, Coors slowly gained a reputation as the best beer west of the Rocky Mountains. For anybody who lived east of the Rockies, the allure of the beer made with pure mountain spring water would remain out of reach. President Gerald Ford was such a fan, he used to smuggle cases of Coors back to the White House. That changed in 1981, when Coors was finally available in all 50 states, and its light version—dubbed the "Silver Bullet"—soon became the fourth best-selling beer in the United States.

1. Some call it grunt work. Others call it Paradise. 2. Beer Legend Arthur Guinness.

GUINNESS LTD.
DUBLIN, IRELAND

ON TAP: GUINNESS, HARP, KILKENNY'S, SMITHWICK. KALIBER

In 1759, a 34-year-old Irish brewer named Arthur Guinness bought the rundown, ramshackle St. James's Gate Brewery for £100 down and £45 a year—for 9,000 years. (Talk about an extended mortgage!) Guinness started brewing a special kind of porter beer and named it after himself. By the turn of the nineteenth century, Guinness was slowly creeping into other ports. An Irish soldier wounded on the battlefield of Waterloo in 1815 later wrote to his family: "When I was sufficiently recovered to be permitted nourishment, I felt the most extraordinary desire for a glass of Guinness, which I knew could be obtained without difficulty. I am confident that it contributed more than anything else to my recovery." Guinness became a favorite of Robert Louis Stevenson, Charles Dickens, and Benjamin Disraeli, and by 1886, the company went public. Over the next hundred years, Guinness would branch into a variety of other businesses: publishing (*The Guinness Book of World Records*—see page 37), resort hotels, wine, even hard liquor. What most people don't realize about Guinness is that it's not an especially strong beer; the dark color denotes the color of the malted grain, not the amount of alcoholic punch. This is how some Dubliners can get away with drinking countless pints per day. Sometimes for breakfast.

THEY LIVE!
ZOMBIE BEERS

Old beers don't always rest in peace. Sometimes, the brand name is purchased by another brewer, reintroduced to the public as a slightly different kind of beer, and sent out to walk among the living once again. I call these "zombie beers."

The Pabst Brewing Company is the George Romero of zombie beers. Pabst has reanimated scores of regional beers (see below). But the biggest surprise is that Pabst no longer brews beer; since 2001, it's been a "beer marketing company." Which means that it farms out the brewing and bottling to other, larger breweries (like Miller, the second-largest brewer in the United States). Here's a look at zombie beers in their prime, and how they're faring in the afterlife.

Oldies but goodies: Vintage cans of Hamm's, Heileman's, and National Bohemian

HAMM'S
HEYDAY: Hamm's was prized for its fresh mountain spring water, its cute, cuddly animated bear spokesman, and its amazing array of signs, ads, clocks, figurines, and displays that filled hundreds of Midwestern taverns.
TODAY: Hamm's is a "price" (cheap) beer brewed by Miller, and a shadow of its former self.

HEILEMAN'S OLD STYLE
HEYDAY: The ultimate Chicago ballpark beer, brewed and consumed by thirsty Midwestern sports fans. Heileman's used to be a respected beer name, right up there with Anheuser, Miller, and Coors. It once even had the world's largest six-pack—six giant storage tanks of beer in LaCrosse, Wisconsin, that held enough Old Style to fill 7,340,796 cans.
TODAY: Pabst markets the beer, simply called Old Style, to Chicago ballparks, but it's not as essential to the game as it used to be.

NATIONAL PREMIUM AND NATIONAL BOHEMIAN

HEYDAY: First brewed in 1885, the National Brewing Company in Baltimore, Maryland, used two animated characters, Mr. Pilsner (for National Premium) and Mr. Boh (for National Bohemian), to help consumers distinguish between the two popular brands. This beer, the ads claimed, hailed from the "land of pleasant living."

TODAY: Marketed by Pabst, National Bohemian has earned the unfortunate nickname "Nasty Boh" on many college campuses.

PIELS

HEYDAY: This famous Brooklyn brewery opened for business on the same day as the Brooklyn Bridge (see page 19). Piels was also famous for being the first to market "draft style" beer in a can.

TODAY: You'll find this beer tucked away with all of the other "price" beers. Pabst also markets this, and it's probably my favorite zombie beer. Piels has "old-man bar" written all over it.

SCHAEFER

HEYDAY: The oldest lager in America, first brewed by Prussian native Frederick Schaefer in 1842. Schaefer was very popular in New York City, especially after the brewery moved to Park Avenue and 51st Street.

TODAY: Another Pabst-marketed beer that stirs memories, but little else.

SCHLITZ

HEYDAY: "The Beer That Made Milwaukee Famous" was famous for "just a kiss of hops." Only 20 years ago, Schlitz was one of the major players, just behind Bud and Miller.

TODAY: Let's say it together: another Pabst-marketed beer. But it could be worse. I bought a 12-pack for $5.49 last year and served it ice-cold to some dinner guests in pilsner glasses. Some actually thought it was microbrew.

SCHMIDT'S

HEYDAY: One of Philadelphia's most famous exports long before Rocky and the cheese steak, Schmidt's was founded by a German emigrant who set up shop in 1860 and started selling ales and porters to working-class drinkers. Schmidt's was a city staple until the brewery dissolved in the mid 1980s.

TODAY: Cans of Schmidt's, now marketed by Pabst, feature shadow outlines of wild animals, and the current beer slogan is the tasteful, "Just Say 'Oh, Schmidt's!'"

STAG

HEYDAY: Very popular in the St. Louis area (Budweiser's backyard), Stag was famous for its commercials featuring Mr. Magoo (Jim Backus), and for offering "golden quality since 1851."

TODAY: Amazingly, Stag hasn't fared too badly in the afterlife; it took home a gold medal in the "Best American-Style Lager" category at the 2001 Great American Beer Festival.

BEER: AN OWNER'S MANUAL

Drinking beer is a basic skill, right? Something you pick up in kindergarten? Not exactly. There's a lot that Mrs. Portnoy didn't teach you about the care, handling, storage, and drinking of beer. It's time for a refresher.

OBTAINING YOUR BEER

The most important thing is to obtain the freshest beer possible. Some brewers make this easy for you, because they give the cans and bottles little "Born On" dates. If the beer you want doesn't have this date, it's time to do a little code cracking.

Often, the code is fairly logical. For instance, all Miller beers—including the ones they contract-brew for Pabst—use an MMDDY code. If today's date is August 1, 2004, and the bottom of your can has the code 07014 (07 = July, 01 = the first, 4 = 2004), then your beer is a month past its prime. You don't even have to check a can for the date; the same code will be on the cardboard box. Check a case before you buy it; the more time a beer has to sit around, the more chances that something will have messed with the flavor.

Of course, the freshest beer possible is draft (or tap) beer. "Draft" (and its British variant, "draught") means "to pull." When beer is pulled straight from the keg, it has less carbonation, which means less of that gassy feeling in your stomach. It also tastes far more crisp, since nothing—no air, no light—has had a chance to mess with the contents. If someone gives me a choice between a bottle of microbrew and a domestic draft beer, I go for the draft, no questions asked.

OPENING YOUR BEER

CAN

Simply hook your finger under the stay tab and gently pull back. If your can doesn't have a stay tab, or even a pull tab, and is just plain metal—because you found it in your grandfather's basement inside a rusty metal cooler with a worn-off Esso Gas advertisement on the side—put the can down. Walk away from the can. Do not attempt to drink the contents of the can.

BOTTLE

If it's a bottle with a twist-off cap, you should theoretically be able to open it with your hand. However, those sharp little ridges on the cap can tear your tender flesh to bits—especially after you've twisted off caps for yourself, your girlfriend, your brother, your mother, and the members of Kiss, who stopped by for the evening. I like to drape a kitchen or bar towel over the top and twist the cap off using that.

If you have a bottle of beer with a regular crown cap, you need an opener—also known as a "church key." If you don't have an opener handy, it's time to play rough.

1. Find a hard surface, such as a big wooden or metal table. Make sure the surface has a reasonably sharp edge.
2. Place the top of your bottle against the table. Be sure the bottom of the crown cap is resting on top of the edge of the table.
3. Smack the flat of your palm against the top of the cap. Aim for the center of the cap.

4. The blow should force the bottle down, while part of the cap will remain caught on the edge of the table, wrenching it from the bottle. If it fails, smack it again—harder.

POURING YOUR BEER

Now that you've opened your bottle or can, here's the most efficient way to transfer the suds to your glass.

1. HOLD YOUR BEER IN ONE HAND AND YOUR GLASS IN THE OTHER. Tilt the glass at a 45-degree angle (fig. a).

2. SLOWLY POUR THE BEER INTO THE GLASS. Make sure that the stream hits the middle of the inside of the glass; it should flow down the rest of the way, which will release carbonation and build a nice head (fig. b). Control is key. After a while, you'll learn to judge how a steady pour will build the head you want.

3. ADJUST THE FLOW. When your glass is about half full, start to return it to its upright position (fig. c). The stream of beer should move away from the side of the glass, and gradually make its way to the center of the glass.

4. ADMIRE THE VIEW. If you've done it slowly and carefully, the beer head should blossom just above the rim of the glass, and the head itself should be two- or three-fingers thick (fig. d).

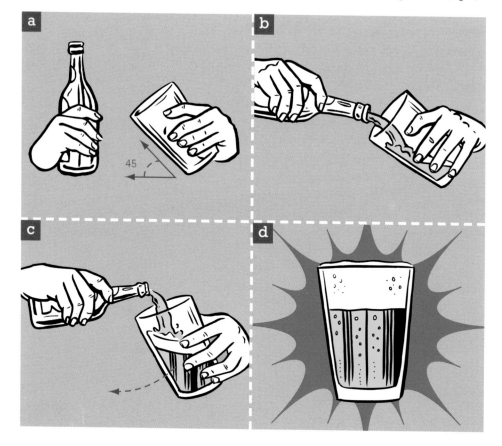

Common Beer-Pouring Mistakes

1. Dumping the beer into the glass like you're pouring water into a car radiator.
2. Pouring straight down the center of the glass, building a monster head you must ungracefully suck away before it overflows and makes a mess.
3. Slamming the glass of beer down on the table, creating a monster head you must ungracefully suck away before it overflows and makes a mess.
4. Missing the glass entirely.

STORING AND CARING FOR YOUR OTHER BEERS

Beer should only be stored in two places: a cool, dark room, or the fridge. Anywhere else, and sunlight or heat can wreak havoc with the precious contents. When loading beers into your fridge, always stand them upright. If you tilt bottles or cans on their side, you'll expose that much more of the beer to the pocket of air inside the bottle. (Hey, every little bit counts.)

The most important rule of all: never freeze your beer, even if it's for only minutes at a time. I used to be guilty of this sin. I'd rush home from the beer store with a case of something I was dying to try, so I'd stick two bottles in the freezer, set the timer on the microwave for 30 minutes, then come back to retrieve my freshly chilled brew. Dumb move. Extreme cold will alter the taste of beer; the delicate balance of grains and hops was not meant to be frozen, then thawed. Now I put my beer in the fridge and wait at least six hours, like a good little boy.

Of course, there's only so much beer space in the average family fridge; my wife insists on storing stuff like milk and orange juice and meat in there, too. One of these days, I'm going to follow in the footsteps of my beloved grandfather and purchase a "beer only" fridge, which I will keep stocked in the basement.

HOW TO ACT LIKE A BEER SNOB

When you drank your first beer, you probably appreciated its unique effects only *after* it left the can, swirled down your throat, and infiltrated your bloodstream. But you missed out on a lot. Anyone aspiring to be a true lover of beer—a *cervezaphile*, as coined by beer historian Gregg Smith—must learn to savor the moments leading up to final bliss. In other words, here's how to sound like a beer snob, in five easy steps.

1. GAZE LONGINGLY AT YOUR BEER

Hold the beer directly in front of you—not up to the light, which will alter its appearance—and try to describe three things: the color of the beer, the color and size of the head, and the consistency (fig. a). The toughest part might be the color; there are only so many synonyms for "straw" and "brown." Try comparing it to a specific object (e.g., "This porter has the dark brown look of a melted Almond Joy candy bar"). And keep your eye on the head; if it quickly dissolves into oblivion, you're probably looking at a flat or cheap beer.

2. SWIRL YOUR BEER

Don't recreate a whirlpool in your glass. Just give it a nice, easy swish to stir things up (fig. b). You'll be amazed at what kinds of aromas the beer will release. Swirling will also test the heartiness of your head; if a gentle swish sends it packing, turn up your nose with displeasure.

3. SNIFF YOUR BEER

Sniff through your nose alone (fig. c), then with your nose and mouth open, then with your nose again. (Your tongue affects how you sense aroma.) Probably the easiest smell to detect is that unpleasant "skunked" factor, which is not unlike opening a 100-year-old tomb and finding a dead animal inside. Beyond that, try to pick out individual aromas, comparing them to specific scents (e.g., "This pale ale smells like a box full of Lemonhead candies").

4. (AT LONG LAST) DRINK YOUR BEER

Go ahead and sip . . . but wait! Don't swallow! Let the beer cascade over your tongue (fig. d), which is divided into specific taste areas: the top (sweetness), the sides (saltiness), the bottom (acids), and the back (bitterness). It's a little easier to detect these flavors if your beer isn't ice cold. You'll be surprised at the number of tastes beer can contain; in my own research, I've tasted caramel, nuts, strawberries, mint, citrus, chicory, chocolate, malt, even banana. It helps to stop thinking of beer as "beer-flavored"—that's the hops talking. Try to focus on what makes this beer distinctive from others. Also, pay attention to the mouthfeel, which is the actual consistency of the beer. Is it thin and wispy, or so thick-bodied that you could cut it with a steak knife?

5. EXPRESS YOURSELF

Put all of your observations together in a couple of pithy sentences (fig. e), and *voilà*! You're on the way to sounding like a complete beer snob. To see some excellent examples of precision beer reviewing, visit www.beeradvocate.com, the Web's largest beer community, run by Todd and

Jason Alström. There are dozens of reviews on pretty much every beer in existence, contributed by members. It's especially amusing to read reviews that cite unique flavors in mass-produced American beer.

The 10 Commandments of a Highbrow Beer Tasting

1. Thou shalt check the freshness of every beer served at the tasting.
2. Thou shalt start with the "lightest" beer (lower alcohol and hop content) first, and work up to more "intense" (higher alcohol and hop content) beers.
3. Thou shalt use the same style of glass—a wide-bodied wine glass—for every beer.
4. Thou shalt not serve beer freezing cold, but not at room temperature, either.
5. Thou shalt cleanse the palate between beers, but not with salty snacks like pretzels or greasy snacks like cheese.
6. Thou shalt eat plain crackers or bread.
7. Thou shalt not suggest "funneling" two or three beer styles, just to move things along.
8. Thou shalt not make fun of a taster who uses a fancy word to describe a flavor. Thou shalt, however, write down that word and use it later to mock the taster.
9. Thou shalt remember that this is supposed to be fun, not a scientific experiment.
10. Thou shalt not remove thy pants at any time during the tasting.

Cheap beer has its place and should not be mocked. If I'm in Smith & Wollensky ordering a filet mignon medium rare, I'm not going to ask the waiter for a can of Schlitz. But if I'm on a long dusty road trip and stumble into the first old-man bar I see, there's nothing better than a glass of whatever's on tap. And if I'm trapped beerless with my wife's family and my brother-in-law suddenly shows up with a thirty-pack of Natural Light, it's like manna from 7-Eleven.

There are a lot of rumors about cheap beer. One is that brands like Natural and Keystone are simply the bottom-of-the-vat remnants of Budweiser and Coors. Not true; they're entirely different batches made from different ingredients. What makes them cheaper? The quality of those ingredients. It costs money to use expensive malted grains, so cheap beers tend to be heavy on the rice and corn. Another rumor is that all cheap beers are actually the same beer with different packaging. This is also untrue—the hangovers and gastrointestinal effects definitely vary.

BALLANTINE ALE

"AMERICA'S LARGEST-SELLING ALE"

Unlike most cheap beers, this is an honest-to-goodness ale, established by Scottish brewer Peter Ballantine back in 1830. It was a pre- and postwar classic, but has since fallen on hard times. Nonetheless, Ballantine earned high marks in an informal survey of college students in a blind taste test for Student.com. "Tastes like it might not even be cheap beer at all!" enthused one tester. "Decent—actually tastes like hops," said another.

GENESEE

"BREWED WITH SIX-ROW BARLEY MALT, CORN GRITS, HOPS FROM THE YAKIMA VALLEY, AND OUR OWN EXCLU-SIVE BOTTOM-FERMENTING YEAST. ALWAYS FULLY KRAUSENED TO PRODUCE CARBONATION NATURALLY FOR A CLEAN, SMOOTH TASTE."

Made by High Falls Brewing Company, Genesee has been a taproom favorite since the turn of the nineteenth century. One of its most unique styles, Genesee Cream Ale, only sounds disgusting; it's actually a fairly refreshing brew. Strangely enough, my father-in-law—who never met a cheap beer he didn't like—says he can't drink Genesee. In an odd way, this is an endorsement.

IRON CITY

"IT'S A 'BURGH THING."

Back in 1899, the Pittsburgh Brewing Company was the third-largest brewer in the United States. Although union trouble in the 1950s tarnished the image of the Steel City's best beer, Iron City is still surprisingly drinkable—which explains why it won a gold medal for American Light Lager at the 1994 Great American Beer Festival.

KEYSTONE

"KEYSTONE LIGHT IS A REFRESHING LIGHT LAGER THAT IS ALWAYS SMOOTH, NEVER BITTER™. KEYSTONE LIGHT IS 4.2 PERCENT ALCOHOL BY VOLUME AND HAS 100 CALORIES PER 12-OUNCE SERVING."

Introduced in 1989 by the Adolph Coors Company, Keystone comes in Light, Ice, and Premium styles. The best I can say about Keystone is that it's inoffensive.

KOCH'S GOLDEN ANNIVERSARY

"A DISTINCTIVE, MODERATELY-HOPPED BEER, 'GOLDEN ANNIE' IS BREWED WITH SIX-ROW PREMIUM MALTS AND A SPECIAL BLEND OF NORTHWESTERN AND IMPORTED HOPS."

Currently brewed by High Falls Brewing Company, the makers of Genesee, Koch's used to have one of the strangest beer labels. It featured a bunch of hops, a pile of grains, and a pilsner glass of beer. But the hops looked uncomfortably like brains, and the grains looked like something unmentionable. Koch would later switch to a much more attractive design: a gold can.

MEISTER BRAU

"MEISTER BRAU IS THE QUALITY FULL-CALORIE BUDGET BEER FROM MILLER BREWING COMPANY BREWED FOR THE COST-CONSCIOUS CONSUMER."

This was the first beer I ever drank—Thanksgiving 1987, courtesy of my parents—and I'm thankful, because it was only uphill from there. The name might be German, but the beer inside is completely American.

MILWAUKEE'S BEST

"USING SELECT PALE MALT, CEREAL
GRAINS, AND YEAST, THIS NATURALLY
HOPPED BEER FEATURES PREMIUM
TASTE, BUT NOT AT A PREMIUM PRICE."

Today it's brewed by Miller, but it originated
in the Adam Gettelman Brewing Company,
which was sold to Miller in 1971. Here's a little-known fact about Adam Gettelman: He
once brewed a beer called "$1,000 Natural
Process"—the brand name was also a stand-
ing offer to anyone who could prove he used something other than malted grains and hops. Come
to think of it, a thousand dollars would probably buy you a lifetime supply of Milwaukee's Best.

NATURAL LIGHT

"A LIGHT BEER WITH A PLEASING AROMA."

Made by Anheuser-Busch, Natty Light is my brother-in-law Tom's favorite cheap beer, mainly
because he believes that it's not too far away from the taste of Budweiser, and a lot less expensive. I've enjoyed a few cans with him at various family holidays, and he has a point. Oddly
enough, plain old Natural doesn't seem to be available anymore.

The Cheapest Beer in America?

The price of beer—like anything else we value—is at the mercy of the economy, as well as
the usual laws of supply and demand. There are other factors, too. Special promotions might
cause the price of a glass to plummet temporarily. Regional beers might be a few cents
cheaper, because they didn't have to travel as far to get to you. Some beers are made with
hops and barley of dubious quality, thus lowering the bottom line.

So what is the cheapest beer in America?

Depends on how you like your cheap beer. The cheapest glass of beer I've ever enjoyed
was a glass of draft Bud for 25 cents at an American Legion Post in Philadelphia. It wasn't
a big glass, but it was ice cold, and it was nice knowing that I could afford two more beers
and a decent tip for under a buck. If you're a cheap-beer fan, find a veteran—your dad, your
grandfather—and become a member. Prices vary per Post; the one my father-in-law attends
recently raised beer prices to 50 cents a glass.

Cheap cases vary by region, and also by promotions. When I was in college, news of the
latest, cheapest case spread like wildfire. Back in 1991, word went out about Koch's Golden
Anniversary, which was selling for $4.99 a case. Of course, some think that beer costing
more than $3.99 a case can't be considered "cheap." Some brave souls have picked up fire-
damaged cases of beer, close-out beers, even St. Patrick's Day green beer in December. If you
make friends with your local beer distributor, you might happen upon some decent bargains
. . . and some truly hideous beer.

OLD MILWAUKEE

"OLD MILWAUKEE IS AMERICA'S BEST-TASTING BEER."

Old Milwaukee was rated "very good" at the 2001 Great American Beer Festival; Old Milwaukee Ice won a silver medal that same year. You probably know this beer from its 1990s-era slogan—It Doesn't Get Any Better Than This™—and commercials featuring the Swedish Bikini Team (see page 180).

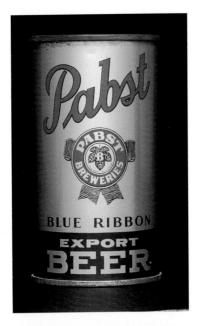

PABST BLUE RIBBON

"THIS IS THE ORIGINAL PABST BLUE RIBBON BEER. NATURE'S CHOICEST PRODUCTS PROVIDE ITS PRIZED FLAVOR. ONLY THE FINEST OF HOPS AND GRAINS ARE USED. SELECTED AS AMERICA'S BEST IN 1893."

It's funny how the whole "blue ribbon" thing started. Originally, PBR was known as "Pabst Select," but Pabst wanted to distinguish itself from the rest of the pack. The company had workers tie fancy blue ribbons around each bottle so patrons could simply ask for "the beer with the blue ribbon." The gimmick caught on, and eventually changed the name of the beer. Today, PBR is enjoying a kind of rebirth among urban hipsters, who like to pair a 16-ounce (470-ml) can with a shot of Jim Beam.

Fill 'Em Up

Years before recyclable bottles and aluminum cans, beer came home in refillable, returnable bottles. You drank the beer, then put the empties right back in the box—which was made with stronger, more durable cardboard. At the end of the week, you'd take your box full of empties back to the beer store, buy a new case, and receive a small rebate in the form of a bottle deposit. The beer was cheaper, and it made environmental sense, too. Today, only 0.2 percent of the beer consumed in America comes from those refillable, returnable bottles, and almost all of that beer is of the cheap, old-man variety. Maybe it's the idea of wrapping our lips around something that has touched the lips of countless drinkers before us; maybe it's laziness. But if you want to experience cheap beer the way your grandfather did—and save about $1.50 in the process—look in the dusty, cobwebbed corners of your favorite beer store. They're there. Waiting for you.

BEER AND FOOD

A couple bottles of beer will sometimes give you the munchies. Why else would college students make a postkegger pizza run at 3 A.M.? It works the other way around, too—some foods just cry out to be accompanied by beer. And in recent years, brewers have been pushing to make beer as much a part of fine cuisine as wine. Who knows? Maybe in a few years, a snooty sommelier will approach you with a fine Belgian lambic resting on his arm.

CLASSIC BAR SNACKS

Some bars are required by state law to serve food. Some bars serve food because the owner is a closet gourmand. Some bars serve free food to keep their customers coming back for more drinks. No matter the reason, food has been paired with beer in bars for hundreds of years, and many interesting combinations have resulted.

FREE LUNCH

To attract customers in the late nineteenth century, tavern owners would offer a "free lunch"—a fairly expansive spread of delectable foods and snacks: slabs of bologna, pickles, nuts, pretzels, radishes, salted fish, cheese. If you wanted to partake, all you had to do was purchase a glass of the tavern's proprietary or favored brand of beer. (For example, if a tavern favored Bud, it was known as a "tied house," since it was "tied" to Anheuser-Busch.)

So what's the catch? You might notice that the items at the "free lunch" tended to be high in salt, which would make customers thirsty, which would encourage them to buy more beer. After the turn of the century, these free lunches were banned, since certain lawmakers believed that this kind of marketing promoted excessive consumption of the "tied" beer. This is where the expression "there's no such thing as a free lunch" originated, and it's also why brewpubs had a hard time establishing themselves. The food wasn't the problem; it was the single, proprietary brand of beer that ran afoul of old "tied house" laws.

You can still find free lunches today, although they're usually offered after work under the guise of a happy hour. When I was fresh out of college and living on my own, I once plotted seven days of happy hour buffets, just so I could eat free for the week.

BEER NUTS®

Raise a glass to Beer Nuts, which just celebrated their 50th birthday in 2003. Beer Nuts are not just any old shelled peanuts found in dingy wooden bowls in every neighborhood tavern; they're a brand name, like Kleenex and Band-Aids. In 1953, the Shirk family candy shop in Bloomington, Illinois, started selling their own mix of peanuts that tasted mostly salty, but with an undercurrent of sweetness. A distributor named Eldridge Brewster convinced the Shirk family to try to market these red-skinned peanuts to bars

The Perfect Lunch: Cheaper than a sandwich, tastier than an energy bar.

and taverns, and dubbed them Beer Nuts. It was a relatively easy sell to bar owners—Beer Nuts were easy to keep around and were salty enough to encourage patrons to order more beer. By the 1970s, the Shirks were shipping 10 million pounds (4.5 million kg) of Beer Nuts to all 50 states, and today they continue to dominate the tavern nut market. The latest addition to the Beer Nuts family is Crunch Nuts, which are peanuts covered in a crunchy, flavored dough.

JARS OF PICKLED EGGS

Remember when I said that certain states require bars to serve food? One popular way around the law is to keep a jar of pickled eggs on a shelf in plain view of Joe Six-Pack. Technically, it's food. Since they remain in their jars, perfectly preserved, for an extended period of time, there's no need to deal with pesky food reorders or inventory or kitchen inspections.

Never been to a bar with a jar of pickled eggs? Then you've never walked on the wild side. There's something special about people who have eaten a pickled egg from a jar with a layer of dust that would rival the Tomb of Tutankhamen. If you're too chicken, you can easily make your own at home. Here's a quick recipe.

WHAT YOU'LL NEED:

- 1 cup (237 ml) cider vinegar
- 1 teaspoon (5 ml) black peppercorns
- 1/2 teaspoon (2.5 ml) whole allspice
- Dash mace
- Dash coriander seeds
- Dash cardamom seeds
- Dash cloves
- 1 small hot red pepper
- 1 1/2 (7.5 ml) teaspoons sugar
- 6 hardboiled eggs

1. In a kettle, combine the vinegar, spices, and sugar.
2. Bring to a boil.
3. Reduce heat, and simmer for 5 minutes.
4. Peel the hardboiled eggs and place in a narrow sterilized jar.
5. Pour the hot liquid over the hardboiled eggs.
6. Place the lid on the jar and let cool.
7. Store in the refrigerator for up to one month.
8. Eat at your own risk.

MATCHING BEER WITH FOOD

There are no rules about matching beer with food; sometimes, a combination will strike you as particularly appealing, such as a Big Mac with a $9 bottle of imported Duvel. But there are some easy guidelines. You should try to make your beer match the food; if you're eating light, go for a lighter beer, like a pilsner; heavy foods deserve heavy beers, like porters and stouts. Also, you can never go wrong by matching your cuisine (Italian, Thai, English, Mexican) with the beers of that country (Birra Moretti, Singha, Newcastle Brown Ale, Negro Modela).

In this chart, I've gathered some food-and-beer matches suggested by a host of beer experts, food writers, good friends, and the guy down at the VFW Post. (He thinks that Pabst Blue Ribbon goes with everything.) These beers are selected either to mirror a taste or to give your taste buds a little balance.

Food	Beer
Barbecued spareribs	India pale ale, stout
Cheeses	Bock, doppelbock, bitter, Trappist beer
Chicken	Märzen and Oktoberfest
Chocolate desserts	Porter
Creamy desserts	Stout
Fresh-baked fruit pies	Lambic
Fried foods	Wheat beer
Glazed ham	India pale ale
Hamburgers and hot dogs	Pilsner
Lamb	French bière de garde
Oysters	Stout
Pizza	Pilsner, ale
Pork	Ale (Irish or American style)
Potato salad	Märzen and Oktoberfest
Sausages	Dark lager
Seafood	Pilsner, pale ale
Shellfish	Dark lager, stout
Smoked meats	Märzen, bock, or smoked beer (*rauchbier*)
Spicy foods	Wheat beer
Steak	Pale ale
After dinner	Barley wine

Foods That Only Taste Good with Beer

- Hard, dark pretzels that are damn near burnt
- Boiled hot dogs
- Mixed nuts
- Sardines in mustard sauce
- Slim Jims®
- Goldfish® (the Pepperidge Farm kind, not the frat house variety)
- Pickled pigs' feet

- White Castle® hamburgers
- A large soft pretzel slathered with cheap mustard
- Nachos with everything on top—and I mean *everything*
- Red-hot Buffalo wings
- Deep-fried turkey

- Oscar Mayer® bologna, right out of the plastic container
- Pickled herring
- Pork rinds
- Popeye's Fried Chicken®
- Fresh kielbasa slices
- Canned pork brains
- Haggis

BEER RECIPES
ENJOY BEER ALL DAY LONG!

Dorothy Parker is credited with the witticism, "Beer: It's not just for breakfast anymore." And she was right—beer can be used for virtually every meal of the day. Wynkoop Brewery's master brewer John Dickenson eats a breakfast of granola, fruit, yogurt, and hot, unhopped wort. Once a month, the owners of the Yuengling Brewery in Pottsville, Pennsylvania, set aside the lunch hour to "test" the latest batch of beer—apparently, a bad one got away from them decades ago (you can never be too careful, you know). And many chefs know that beer makes an excellent marinade and meat tenderizer: Simply poke some holes in your cut of meat, soak it in a bowl full of English ale, refrigerate for a few hours, and the result will be a tender cut of beef that retains its original flavor.

For your enjoyment, here are four other beer recipes that can be enjoyed throughout the day. You might not want to try all of these in the same day; then again, maybe you will.

BREAKFAST: SWEET POTATO BUBBLE-AND-SQUEAK

Courtesy of my old colleague Denis Boyles at www.modernman.com. The sweet potato contributes significantly to the taste and blends well with the ale. Serve it for breakfast, and you won't have to eat again until lunchtime.

WHAT YOU'LL NEED:

- ¼ pound (115 g) Brussels sprouts, peeled and diced
- 1 medium red-skinned sweet potato, peeled and diced
- 1 large potato, peeled, and diced
- 1 medium onion, peeled and diced
- ¼ teaspoon (1 ml) freshly ground black pepper
- Salt
- 1 half-pint (176 ml) of ale
- Pat of butter
- 2 poached eggs

1. Place Brussels sprouts, sweet potato, potato, and onion in a large pot and add water to cover. Boil on high heat for 15 to 20 minutes or until soft.
2. Drain and transfer to a large bowl.
3. Mash it all up using a fork or potato masher. Season with pepper and salt to taste.
4. Stir in the ale and set aside.
5. Melt the butter in a skillet over medium-high heat. Form the vegetable mixture into two patties approximately half an inch thick and add to the skillet. Fry for 10 minutes or until lightly brown.
6. Turn the patties over and brown the other side for another 10 minutes.
7. Serve hot, topped with the poached eggs.

LUNCH: CHICKEN IN ALE

People have been mixing chicken and beer for years. Here's a can't-miss variation on a time-honored tradition.

WHAT YOU'LL NEED:
- Juice of one lemon
- 2 cups (473 ml) pale ale
- 1 teaspoon (5 ml) diced garlic
- 2 tablespoons (30 ml) olive oil
- 1 tablespoon (15 ml) chopped parsley
- 1 teaspoon (5 ml) Tabasco sauce
- 1 teaspoon (5 ml) soy sauce
- 12 crushed peppercorns
- 4 chicken thighs
- Baby spinach leaves

1. Mix the first eight ingredients—lemon juice through peppercorns—to make the marinade. Place in large shallow dish. Add the chicken and turn to coat with the marinade.
2. Cover with plastic wrap and refrigerate for at least 8 hours.
3. Remove the chicken from the marinade and cook on a preheated grill for approximately 15 minutes a side, basting frequently with marinade until the chicken is cooked through. Discard the remaining marinade.
4. Arrange on a serving dish and garnish with spinach.

DINNER: GUINNESS GAMMON AND SPINACH

This delightful meal came to me from the good people at the Guinness brewery—who else would serve up a meal of beer and gammon?

WHAT YOU'LL NEED:
- 4 pounds (1.8 kg) center-leg cut of pale ham
- 1 cup (237 ml) brown sugar
- 2 cups (473 ml) Guinness
- 6 whole cloves
- Fresh spinach
- 1 lemon, cut into wedges

1. Leave the bone in the ham and soak overnight in cold water.
2. Drain, then place the ham in a deep pot with the sugar, Guinness, and cloves. Add enough water to cover, then bring to a boil and simmer for one hour.
3. Remove the ham from the liquid, slice, and serve with spinach and wedges of lemon.

DESSERT: BEER ICE CREAM

Our final recipe comes courtesy of Lucy Saunder and her web site, www.beercook.com. Yes, I've tried it. And yes, it's fantastic.

WHAT YOU'LL NEED:
- 1 quart (.95 l) coffee ice cream
- 1 cup (237 ml) stout
- 1 cup (237 ml) grated dark semisweet chocolate

1. Soften the ice cream in the microwave for about 20 seconds.
2. Scoop the ice cream into the bowl of a large stand mixer, and add the stout and grated chocolate. Mix well.
3. Pour into 1-cup (237-ml) ice cream dishes and refreeze for 4 hours.
4. When you serve your guests, make sure to supply a bottle of the same stout you used making the ice cream.

The Phenomenon of Beer-Can Chicken

I don't want to know who first tried milk; I just know it was a brave soul. Likewise, I'm not sure I want to know who first had the idea to shove a can of beer up a dead chicken's backside and pop it onto the grill.

But someone did, and the technique has become wildly popular on the barbecue circuit. Grilling expert Steven Raichlen even devoted an entire book to the topic—his *Beer-Can Chicken: And 74 Other Offbeat Recipes for the Grill* is a comprehensive look at this bizarre grilling technique. The idea is that a can of beer, stuck inside a chicken, will imbue the bird with juicy flavor, while its outside will become delightfully crisp.

Raichlen has his own version, as do other grilling enthusiasts. But here's a quick and dirty version: To make your own beer-can chicken, you'll need a medium-size whole bird, salt, pepper, Worcestershire sauce, and, of course, a can of beer. Make sure it's a 12-ounce (355-ml) aluminum can with no seams. Open the can of beer and drink half. Now, cut off the top third of the can (or use a church key to puncture more holes on top) and add 1 teaspoon (5 ml) of salt, 1 teaspoon (5 ml) of pepper, and 1 teaspoon (5 ml) of Worcestershire sauce.

Now shove the can you-know-where, and place the bird on top of your grill so it looks like it's standing. Fire up the flames to medium, and let it cook for about an hour on the open grill. The brew inside will boil, evaporate, and infuse your bird with flavor. Throw the can away before eating the chicken.

BREW IT YOURSELF

Ah, the thrill of creating your own beer—it's as close as you can come to playing God without stitching together body parts and messing with lightning. Nothing beats home-brew lessons from a master brewer, or even a solid book on the subject. But if you're curious about how much time, effort, and money it takes to brew your own beer, here's a quick overview.

1. BRUSH UP ON YOUR CHEMISTRY.

To understand the basic principles of home brewing, it helps to understand the miracle of fermentation. In a nutshell, yeast is a living organism that—at the right temperature—converts sugar into carbon dioxide and alcohol. As a brewer, your job is to facilitate this process. Take a look at "The Physics and Chemistry of Beer" on page 151 and come back here when you're finished.

2. BUY SOME HOME-BREW GEAR.

All told, this equipment should set you back $150 to $200. You can jury-rig certain items from household materials, but you're probably better off buying everything from a home-brew shop you trust.

3. PICK A RECIPE AND BUY THE INGREDIENTS.

First-timers should purchase a ready-made "beer kit" that includes all of the necessary ingredients—including a can of hopped malt concentrate, a packet of yeast, and some "fermentables," such as brewer's sugar, malt extract, Demerara sugar, or rice syrup. The more fermentables you add, the more your beer will ferment, which increases the alcohol content. Advanced beer recipes can be every bit as complex and rewarding as recipes for a gourmet meal.

4. CLEAN AND SANITIZE YOUR GEAR.

Believe it or not, this is the most important step in the whole process. You need to sanitize everything that will make contact with the beer—pots, utensils, hoses, air locks, bottles, everything. Just one strain of bacteria or fungus can completely ruin your whole batch. Commercial sanitizers are available from any home-brewing supply store, or you can dump the equipment in the dishwasher and run it on the "heat dry" cycle. Still another option is to soak your supplies in a solution of bleach and water for 30 minutes; this is all but guaranteed to destroy any nastiness lurking about. Whatever your method, be sure to rinse everything with cold water when you're finished, and let the equipment air-dry.

5. COOK YOUR INGREDIENTS.

This will vary depending on your equipment, but you'll typically fill your brewpot with 2 quarts of water and bring it to a boil. Add your beer kit ingredients and stir briskly, making sure everything dissolves. Lower the heat to simmer, pop the lid on, and let it cook for 15 minutes.

Next, take your primary fermenter and fill it with 4 gallons (15 l) of cold water. Pour in your hot beer kit mixture. Mix well so that oxygen will permeate the mix. When the temperature reaches 70 to 80 degrees Fahrenheit (21.1 to 26.7 degrees Celsius), it's time to add the yeast (now you know why you bought that thermometer). Congrats. You've made wort—the stuff that will eventually ferment.

6. WAIT FOR THE WORT TO FERMENT.

An-ti-ci-paaaaaaation. Fermenting can take anywhere from three to five days or more. You can tell the wort is fermenting by the little white bubbles that form in the air lock. Fermenting is like microwaving popcorn; if the bubbles are popping up fast and furious, it's too soon to stop the process. But if the action slows to the point where there's a good two minutes between bubbles, primary fermentation is probably complete. (You'll want to wait, though; bottling a beer that is still fermenting can result in messy explosions of primordial wort.)

7. SIPHON THE BEER FROM THE FERMENTER INTO A BOTTLING BUCKET.

By now, your fermenting vat has a bunch of settled yeast at the bottom—this sludge will cloud your beer and spoil its taste. So you'll need to use rubber tubing to siphon off the beer. This gets a little tricky, so bear with me. First, place the fermenter on a shelf that is higher than your bottling bucket. Next, fill the siphon tubing with water (fig. a) and hold it in a U shape, with a finger covering either end (fig. b). Place one end of the tube in the fermented wort. Remove your finger just before dipping it in (fig. c). Don't lower the tube too close to the bottom of the bucket, or it'll suck out the sludge. Place the other end of the tube in the bottling bucket and release your finger (fig. d). The water will drain out of the tube, into the bottling bucket, and the beer will follow it along.

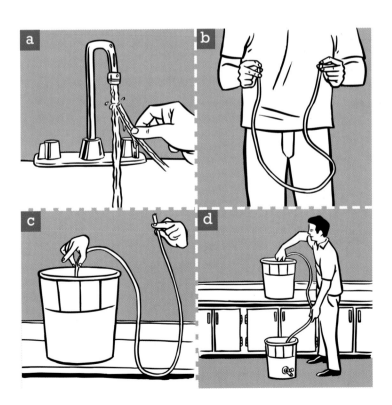

8. BOTTLE IT UP.

Most brew kits will advise you to pour a solution of pure dextrose into the bottling bucket—this will help carbonate your beer. But don't take a sip just yet—you need to get the beer in bottles, where it will finish the fermentation process. Make sure your bottles are squeaky clean—your old empties can have a lot of moldy goo if they've been sitting around. Use a commercial sanitizer or the bleach and water method described in step 4. Once they're clean, use the spout at the bottom of the bottling bucket to pour the beer into individual bottles.

9. CAP AND STORE.

Leave an inch of air at the top of each bottle and cap as soon as you can, using either twist-ons, self-sealing bottles, or a capping machine. The quicker you can get your newborn beer away from the air, the better. Put all of your bottles in a cool place—between 60 and 70 degrees Fahrenheit (15.6 and 21.1 degrees Celsius); a basement usually does the trick. And now you have to wait for secondary fermentation to occur, which usually takes about one or two weeks. Hey, it's better than pregnancy.

10. BOTTOMS UP.

When the cloudiness (caused by yeast) in your beer starts to clear, you'll know your brew is ready to be served. Chill some bottles in the refrigerator and invite some friends over. You might want to take a test sip first, of course. That way, if the batch is lousy, you can replace your home brew with Sam Adams, and your friends will be none the wiser.

Clonebrews

I was kidding about presenting Sam Adams as your own work. But some home brewers actually try to match their beers to commercial beers. The subgenre is called "clonebrewing," and it's almost like hacking a beer. The acknowledged masters of clonebrewing are Tess and Mark Szamatulski, who have written two books, *Clonebrews* and *Beer Captured*—both are full of detailed recipes that mimic Samuel Adams, Foster's, and Sierra Nevada, among others. Their research involves plenty of trial and error—namely, tweaking grains and mashes and water until the beer starts to taste like the commercial version. Cynics may say that it's a helluva lot of work for something you can pick up at the grocery store for $20, but it's also a great way to learn about what makes your favorite beer taste so damn good.

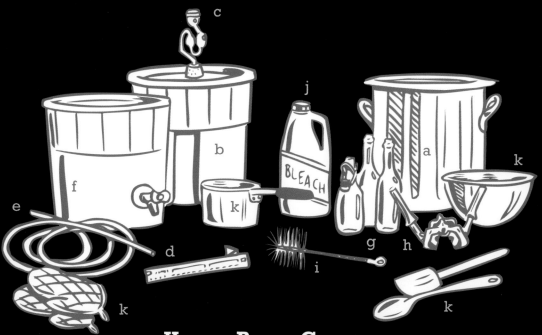

Home-Brew Gear

a **BREWPOT:** Make sure it's at least 16 quarts (15 l), and made of stainless steel or enamel-coated metal.

b **PRIMARY FERMENTER:** Where the magic happens. Look for one that's at least 7 gallons (26.5 l), and made with "food-grade" plastic (this will keep airborne nastiness out of your fermenting beer).

c **AIR LOCK AND STOPPER:** This gizmo fits on your primary fermenter; it helps keep that airborne nastiness out, and allows carbon dioxide to escape—otherwise, your beer would become a bomb.

d **STICK-ON THERMOMETER:** You'll attach this to the side of your primary fermenter to see how things are going inside.

e **PLASTIC HOSE:** Five feet (1.5 m) of food-grade plastic hose to carry your beer from one place to another. Do not use your old garden hose, unless you want your beer to taste like onion weed.

f **BOTTLING BUCKET:** This must also be made of food-grade plastic, and be as big as your primary fermenter, since this bucket is a way station for your beer before it makes it into your bottles.

g **BOTTLES AND CAPS:** Where you'll store your home brew until it reaches your stomach. You can use empties, as long as they have smooth tops (no twist-off grooves) and are made of dark glass. Some home brewers buy cases of Grolsch, since they have those nifty self-capping tops, just to use the bottles.

h **BOTTLE CAPPER:** The device you use to affix bottle caps to your bottle. Go for the kind you can operate with one hand, so your other is free to hold the bottle.

i **BOTTLE BRUSH:** To clean your bottles, just as you would clean a baby bottle.

j **COMMERCIAL SANITIZER OR BLEACH:** For the all-important task of cleaning your gear.

k **ASSORTED HOUSEHOLD ITEMS:** A small bowl, a saucepan, a rubber spatula, a stainless steel mixing spoon, and oven mitts that look like the heads of cows or pigs. (Use the animal mitts to amuse yourself while waiting for your beer to ferment.)

BEER CRAFTS AND GEAR

"May your glass be ever full. May the roof over your head be always

strong. May you be in heaven half an hour before the devil knows

you're dead."—*Old Irish Toast*

If you're looking for beer, you've come to the wrong place. This chapter doesn't have a drop of it. Sure, you'll find beer glasses, beer mugs, beer steins, beer chalices, beer funnels, beer kegs, beer-cap dogs, beer-can houses, beer hats, beer games, beer airplanes, and beer insects. But no beer. Sorry to disappoint you. For beer, turn to any other section of this book. Thank you for your cooperation.

AW, YOU MUGS

MUGS

Of all the glassware in the world, why have mugs become synonymous with beer? Because they sure beat drinking beer out of two cupped hands. Humans have been brewing beer for thousands of years, and we haven't always had fancy pilsner glasses or Spuds MacKenzie glass pints. The most common drinking vessels used to be bowls, and later, cups. Slapping a handle on a vessel made it a "mug"—which is a Scandinavian term that's related to "jug." "Mug" is also synonymous with a grotesque, exaggerated face, and many early mugs were adorned with such faces.

These days, thankfully, mugs no longer resemble Bea Arthur with a hangover. Mugs are collected, prized, displayed, and, more importantly, used in homes and bars across the country. Check out some of these classics.

Mugged at Your Local Bar

If your favorite watering hole serves draft beer in glass mugs thicker than Anna Nicole Smith, beware. You're probably being tricked into thinking you're receiving a decent-sized amount of beer (12 ounces [330 ml]), when you're actually receiving a pitiful amount of beer (8 ounces [220 ml]). Don't let anyone tell you that the thicker glass keeps your beer colder for a longer period of time, either—thick glass conducts the heat from your hand just as quickly as thin glass. Maybe it's time you found another watering hole. Or at least started bringing your own glassware from home.

Guinness
Stout

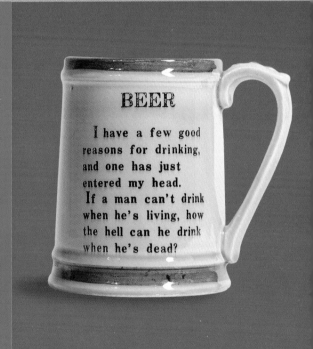

I only drink
to make
other people
more interesting

BEER

I have a few good
reasons for drinking,
and one has just
entered my head.
If a man can't drink
when he's living, how
the hell can he drink
when he's dead?

FRANKEN-STEINS

If you like drinking beer from one of those elaborate, ridiculously large German beer steins, you can thank the bubonic plague. Back in the fourteenth century, with the plague as rampant as the "Electric Slide" at weddings, it was wise to cover your food and drink whenever possible. Beer was no exception, and traditional beer mugs soon developed lids. Some clever wag came up with a cap mechanism that could be triggered with one thumb, opening the lid to reveal the beer inside when its holder wanted a swallow. The lid is what separates a stein—short for the German word *steinzeugkrug*, which means "stoneware jug"—from an ordinary beer mug.

This nifty advance in beer spawned another breakthrough: stoneware, which is basically ordinary clay heated to extremely high temperatures, resulting in a very durable and sanitary stein. Such advances didn't come cheap; steins were expensive. But that meant they were also worthy of some really elaborate art, and boy, did those Germans (and later, English) have a field day. Some steins tell elaborate stories; others depict the twelve apostles of Christ; still others show entire castles, towns, or cities. The best steins pack in more action than a Jerry Bruckheimer flick.

To Chill, or Not to Chill?

Some people keep a glass mug in the freezer so it's nice and frosty when they go to pour themselves a beer. Here are two reasons not to do this: First, if your mug is frosty and icy on the outside, it's going to be that way on the inside, which means you'll wind up with miniature icebergs floating in your beer. This will dilute the flavor. Second, if you keep your beer in a fridge, it's already cold, anyway. Are you planning on nursing that bad boy for two hours? If so, skip the beer and order something that'll keep, like a Shirley Temple.

THE PERFECT GLASS FOR EVERY BEER

Why should you bother pouring your beer into a fancy glass? Because doing so will give it a chance to breathe, releasing flavors and aromas that might not be detectable if you suck it right from the bottle. And don't underestimate the eye-candy factor. There's nothing more beautiful than a perfectly poured golden pilsner with a head that's as soft and white as the clouds of heaven.

Still not convinced? Keep in mind that bottled and canned beer is a highly gaseous beverage. Pour it into a glass, and much of the gas will be released—which means it won't have to enter your body before seeking release, you dig? Here's how to pair your favorite beer with the glass of its dreams.

1. MUG
PERFECT FOR . . . ALES, LAGERS, AND OKTOBERFESTS
A solid choice. The only drawback is that unless you opt for a stein, a mug will never hold as much beer as a pint glass. But it's a very social drinking vessel, since it can withstand numerous toasts and clinks.

2. PINT
PERFECT FOR . . . MOST LAGERS, ALES, PORTERS, AND STOUTS
Old reliable. Pint glasses come in both 16-ounce (440-ml) and 20-ounce (550-ml) "Imperial" sizes. You can recognize the Imperial style by the weird bulge at the top. Imperial pints are good for beers with spectacular foamy heads, or for people who prefer to drink 20 ounces (550 ml) of beer instead of just 16 ounces (440 ml).

3. PILSNER
PERFECT FOR . . . YOU-KNOW-WHATS AND WHEAT BEERS
Pilsner beer is the only beer style with its own glass. Most mass-produced American beers (Bud, Miller, Coors) are pilsners, and all of them are vastly improved when poured into a proper pilsner glass. These glasses are slender at the bottom and wider on top to help maintain a strong head.

Caring for Your Beer Glass

Don't stick your beer glasses in the dishwasher. Dishwashing detergent will leave behind a film, and that film will screw with your beer. Instead, hand wash your prized glasses and let them air-dry (lint and dust from towels will also screw with your beer). Hard-core aficionados even recommend that you use a separate rag or sponge to wash your beer glassware, because faint particles of food or grease from your usual rag will also screw with your beer. You don't want things screwing with your beer, do you?

4. FLUTE
PERFECT FOR . . . LAMBICS AND FRUIT LAMBICS

Lambics are a bit of an aberration; you'll want these bubbly beers to retain as much of their carbonation as possible. The elegant design of the flute does exactly that (which is why people also sip champagne from them).

5. GOBLET
PERFECT FOR . . . BELGIAN-STYLE BEERS, BARLEY WINE, AND OTHER HEAVY ALES

Goblets are the brandy-snifters of the beer world, best reserved for strong, powerful ales that need a little twirling (like brandy) to release aroma and flavor. These don't hold much beer, but then again, you don't need much heavy ale to send you on your way.

6. CHALICE
PERFECT FOR . . . TRAPPIST AND ABBEY DUBBELS AND TRIPLES

This is the fanciest beer vessel going, and it's meant for the fanciest beers—dubbels and triples, which are descriptions of the beer's malt strength. (Dubbels are "double" the malt strength, and so on.) The vessel is designed to trap a 1-inch (2.5 cm) head, which in turn traps the flavor. Drink beer from a chalice, and most beer drinkers won't even know you're drinking beer.

7. YARD GLASS
PERFECT FOR ... DRINKING 2 LITERS OF BEER AT A TIME

Yards were first enjoyed by eighteenth-century coachmen, who weren't allowed to leave their coaches while their passengers made merry at the village inn. So barmaids would bring the driver a yard of beer, which was tall enough to be handed up to him and deep enough to get him through a long night. Today, yard glasses are a decadent, more socially acceptable version of a beer funnel (see below).

8. FUNNEL
PERFECT FOR ... GETTING BLITZED

Every college dorm or apartment has one of these tucked away somewhere, caked in dried foam and tacky residue. It's comprised of a funnel connected to a plastic tube, which may or may not have a fancy valve built into it. (If not, you hold your finger over the other end of the tube.) Once released, the funnel can deliver 12 ounces (355 ml) of beer in less than 4 seconds—if you don't gag halfway through.

9. OPAQUE PLASTIC CUP
PERFECT FOR ... KEG BEER ON YOUR BACK LAWN

Spend the extra dollar and buy the fancy, extra-durable acrylic cups. These will cut down on the foam. Plus, you can also rinse and reuse them, which means you'll have fewer plastic cups to pick out of the lawn the next morning.

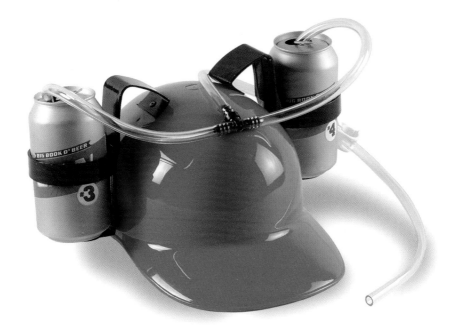

10. GOOFY PLASTIC CAP WITH BEER TUBES
PERFECT FOR . . . MAKING AN ASS OF YOURSELF IN PUBLIC

This is the novelty beer-delivery system that refuses to die, and I hope it never does. It speaks of American ingenuity, efficiency, and engineering. Plus, there's no other drinking vessel in the world that allows you to drink two different beers at the same time.

Erdinger Champ: We Don't Need No Stinkin' Opener!

I thought I was picking up just another cool German wheat beer—Erdinger Champ—when I felt the odd cog-like indentations on the bottom of the bottle. That's when I discovered perhaps the coolest beer bottle innovation since tinted glass: a built-in opener. No church key or bar opener needed; the cog-shaped bottom fits perfectly around the cap on another bottle of Erdinger Champ. Simply dock the two bottles together, twist, return the favor on the other bottle, then enjoy. Erdinger's Web site boasts that "The twist-opener is also a great way of hooking up with other Erdinger Champ drinkers." Emphasis on the "hooking up," no doubt.

BEER KEGS AND KEGERATORS

THE INCREDIBLE, DELECTABLE KEG

Nothing beats a beer poured straight from the keg. Sunlight hasn't touched a precious molecule of this beer since the day it was brewed. There are no preserving chemicals and no pasteurization. It's the freshest beer you can get, short of breaking into your favorite brewery and scooping out a pint for yourself.

Kegs come in two basic sizes: a "half" and a "quarter" (or "pony"). A keg, half a barrel of beer, is 15.5 gallons (58.9 l), or 165 glasses. A quarter keg is 7.75 gallons (29.5 l), about 83 glasses. For more beer math, see page 161.

There are two important rules with kegs: Never shake them up, and never let them get warm. The first rule is easy, if you remember that "Roll Out the Barrel" is a *figure of speech*. Never, ever roll a keg of beer, even if it's just from your car to your back deck. Recruit a friend and lift using the handles. That's why they're built into the sides.

To keep the keg cold, you'll need a large container (a trash can will do) and a lot of ice. Treat the keg like an internal organ that's recently been harvested: Completely surround it with ice, especially on the bottom and sides.

KEGERATORS (AKA KEG REFRIGERATORS)

My father-in-law bought his keg refrigerator in 1982, and he's never looked back. Now, there's something you need to understand about my father-in-law—he has lousy taste in beer. He won't touch a Sam Adams with a stick, and he even dismisses most lager-style beers as "too fancy." Instead, he prefers the cheap, mass-produced stuff. So when he offers me a brew from the half-fridge in the basement, I think twice. But if he offers me a cold one from the kegerator, I practically jump out of my chair to go fetch it. It's that good—even the swill he drinks—coming from the kegerator.

What's the magic? Basically, a kegerator is the home version of the beer-dispensing devices you find in bars. It features a carbon dioxide (CO_2) tank that keeps the beer under constant pressure and guarantees a nice, fresh head with every serving. (You need to replace the CO_2 after five or six kegs.) Prices run anywhere from $500 (if you catch a sale) to $2,000 or more. It's a serious investment, in terms of both money and beer. In other words, you'd better enjoy what you put on tap, because that will be your next 165 beers.

1. Stocking up for happy hour at the Temple Bar. 2. A scene from a 1969 keg party. 3. The ultimate appliance for serious beer drinkers.

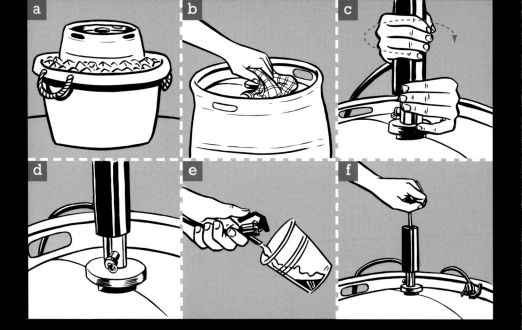

How to Tappa Kegga Beer

1. Let the keg settle for 1 hour after bringing it home (fig. a).
2. Clean off the tap area (the circular "docking port" on top) with a clean wet rag. If you don't, the seal won't be tight, and that will result in foam. Foam is not good (fig. b).
3. Put the tap on the top of the keg and turn until it locks down in the notches. Turn it hard, so it's nice and flat against the lip. Everything should be locked in. Nothing should wobble (fig. c).
4. See that little metal stub at the bottom of the tap? Push it. That will release pressure inside and reduce foam. Again, foam is not good (fig. d).
5. Aim the tap head toward the middle of the cup and pour. It's normal for the first three beers to be foamy. But after the fourth beer, the foam factor should go way down. If it doesn't, you probably don't have a tight seal. Unlock it and try again (fig. e).
6. Pump the keg when you feel the stream of heavenly suds starting to slow. Pour while you pump, so you know when to stop (in other words, when the beer is flowing strong again) (fig. f).

BEER CRAFTS

When the last drop of beer has been consumed, the fun isn't over. Instead of pitching those cans, bottles, caps, or coasters into the nearest recycling bin, you can use them to create all kinds of wonderful home crafts. In fact, you can even use them to create an actual home (see page 136). Here are five projects to get you started.

BEER-COASTER POSTCARDS

An activity for the craft-challenged—there's very little "crafting" involved. Simply take a beer coaster (square ones work best) and treat it like a postcard. Write your buddy or loved one a message on the back, slap on a stamp, include the address, and be sure to stress how much you're enjoying the beer wherever you happen to be. Coasters are accepted by most post offices around the world, and they have the additional benefit of being useful to their recipient.

BEER-CAP DOG

Another good one for beginners—almost as easy as stringing popcorn around a Christmas Tree.

WHAT YOU'LL NEED:

- 78 metal beer caps
- Drill (or a hammer and nail)
- Hot glue gun
- Glue sticks
- Thin-gauge wire
- Heavy-duty scissors
- 3 buttons
- Pliers

Man's best friend: Seventy-eight beer caps in the shape of a dog.

1. Drill a small hole through the middle of 75 caps. (Or use a hammer and nail to make the holes.)
2. Thread wire through the holes to create five different strings of caps. For the head and body, use 35 caps. For the two front legs, create two strings of 9 caps. For the rear legs, create two strings of 11 caps.
3. At the ends of each string, bend the wire and use a dab of glue to secure it to the end caps.
4. Glue the legs to the body. Add buttons to create the eyes and nose.
5. Bend the remaining caps in half with the pliers, and glue them on to create the ears and tail.

It's a fact: Aluminum is the recommended gift for ten-year wedding anniversaries.

BEER-CAN VOTIVE CANDLE HOLDER

What's more romantic than sitting in your favorite recliner and drinking a cold one? Sitting in your favorite recliner and drinking a cold one by *candlelight*.

WHAT YOU'LL NEED:

- Beer can
- Sandpaper
- Votive candle
- Tracing paper
- Heavy-duty scissors
- Gloves
- Can opener
- Drill (or a hammer and nail)
- Pencil

1. Use sandpaper to dull the aluminum and give the can a nice distressed look.
2. Remove the top of the can with the can opener (fig. a).
3. Trace the outline shown on the opposite page on a sheet of tracing paper. Cut the tracing paper to the shape of the template.
4. Wrap the template around the bottom of the can and attach with tape (fig. b).
5. Trace the outline onto the can with the pencil (fig. c).
6. Put on the gloves (to protect yourself) and cut around the edge of the outline.
7. Curve the scallops forward or backward as you desire.
8. Use the drill (or the hammer and nail) to poke a hole in each scallop (fig. d).
9. Insert candle (fig. e). For additional embellishments, consider adding glass beads, small pebbles, or colored sand (as shown above).

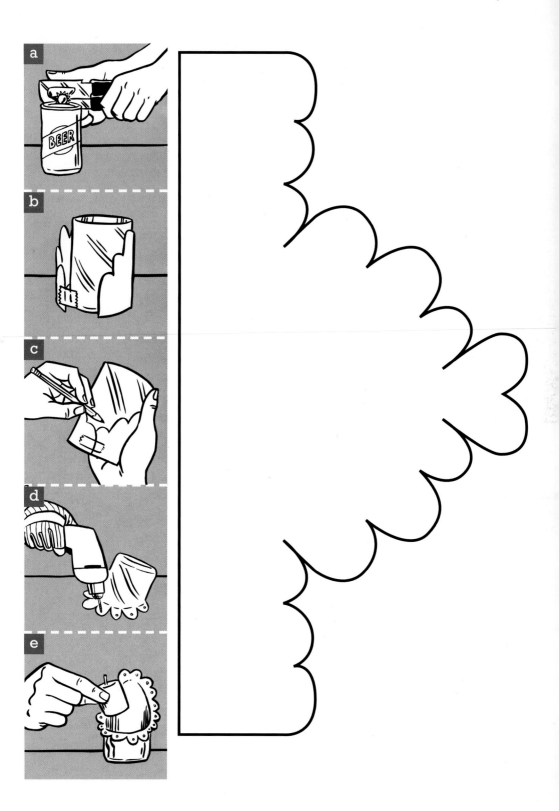

Caution: Hat may leave tiny nicks and cuts in user's forehead.

BEER-CAN HAT

People have been making crocheted hats using beer cans since the 1960s, and they're just as fly today as they were 40 years ago. Now, I don't know how to crochet, but fortunately my friend Erin Slonaker does. And after drinking a sixer of Pabst Blue Ribbon for inspiration (and materials), she crocheted the magnificent piece of headwear that you see in the above photograph.

WHAT YOU'LL NEED

- 3 beer cans (pliable for cutting)
- 1 X-acto knife
- 2 skeins of worsted weight yarn (in different colors)
- Hook size G or H
- Heavy-duty scissors
- Yarn needle
- 1 1/4-inch hole punch
- 1 tapestry needle

Even beginners can make this hat. We've included a sketch of double crochet and treble stitch, in case you need some help with those stitches.

1. Cut out the beer can labels (2 from each can). Punch 16 evenly spaced holes around the label, approximately half an inch away from the edge.
2. With color A, chain stitch (ch) once, leaving a tail 6 to 7 inches long. Double crochet

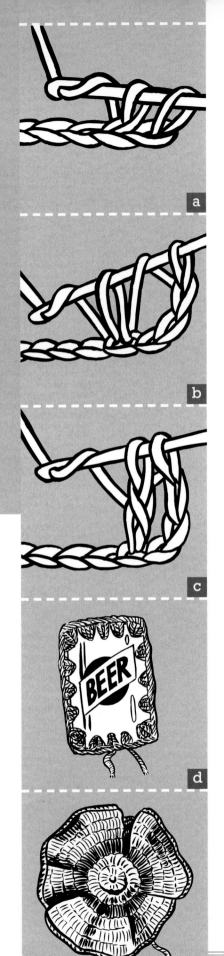

(dc, fig. a) 3 times in each hole along the edges; dc 5 times in the corners (fig. d). Slip stitch (sl st) into the first stitch, then break the yarn. Work the rest of the labels in the same way.

3. Thread the tapestry needle with the tail on one label, and sew one long side to the long side of another can (side to side). Repeat until all labels are connected side to side to form a ring.

4. With color A, ch 1, then join and single crochet (sc) once into each stitch along the top of the ring, twice between each oval until the end, then sl st into the first stitch and the break yarn.

5. To make the top of the hat: With color B, ch 5 stitches and then sl st into the first chain to form a ring.

Row 1: Ch 3 (acts as one treble stitch), then treble stitch (tr, figs. b and c) 13 times into the ring. Sl st into top of ch to complete the circle (14 stitches).

Row 2: Ch 3, then tr 2 into top of each tr. Sl st to complete the circle (28 stitches).

Row 3: Ch 3, then tr 2 into the top of each tr. Sl st to complete the circle (56 stitches).

Row 4: Ch 3, then tr 2 into the top of each tr. Sl st to complete the circle (112 stitches).

Row 5: Ch 3, then *tr 1 into the top of next 7, tr 2 in next stitch, and repeat from *. Sl st to complete the circle (126 stitches).

(Man's hat—Row 6: Ch 3, then tr 1 around.)

The hat will be ruffled (fig. e).

6. To join the crown and sides of the hat, sl st around with color A.

7. To make the hat brim: With color B, ch 3, then tr 1 into each stitch along the bottom of the labels, tr 2 between each label. Sl st to complete the circle.

8. Ch 3, then tr 1 into each stitch. Sl st to complete the circle. Repeat for four more rows. Break the yarn and weave the tail in.

THE SWIERCZYNSKI BEER-CAP TABLE

If you take the time and effort to construct this beer-cap table—originally designed in the late 1970s by my father, Walter Swierczynski, while Santana albums blared in the background—you'll have a family heirloom that will outlive your children and your children's children. Ours is 20-plus years old and still going strong.

WHAT YOU'LL NEED

This table consists mostly of two by fours (which, as any woodworker will tell you, actually measure 3¹/2 by 1¹/2 inches—go figure). You'll need a total of 16 pieces:

- 4 20" cuts (end rails)
- 4 13" cuts (end rails)
- 8 47" cuts (base and side rails)

PLUS. . .

- 1 piece of plywood, 18" x 47" and a half-inch thick
- 1 box of #12 (3¹/2 inch) screws
- 1 box of 2-inch finishing nails
- Drill
- Router
- Wood stain
- Polyurethane
- Epoxy
- Plenty of flat beer bottle caps
- Wood putty

1. Assemble the base. The base consists of six 47" pieces attached with #12 screws. Take one 47" piece and use a half-inch bit to drill four holes halfway into the piece. Place the wood alongside another 47" piece. Insert a #12 screw into each hole and screw it through the rest of the wood, binding the two pieces together (fig. a). Repeat this process for all of the screws and all of the pieces. When finished, you should have one piece—made up of those six pieces—that is 47" long and 21" wide. It should look like a raft.

2. Assemble the end rails. Each end rail consists of two 20" pieces and two 13" pieces. On one of those 13" pieces—the one that will be on top—you'll need to use a router to make a ¹/2" by ¹/2" notch across the entire length (this notch will eventually support the tabletop). Assemble the four pieces as shown below, and attach using the recessed screw technique described in Step 1 (fig. b).

3. Attach the end rails to the base. Assemble the end rails and base as shown below, and

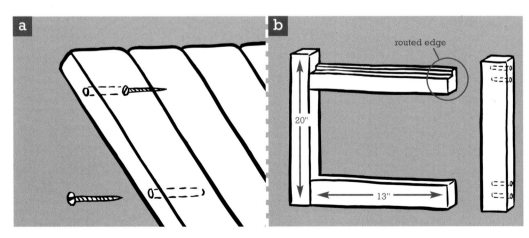

attach using 8 evenly spaced screws on either side (fig. c).

4. Attach the side rails. Take your remaining two pieces of 47" cuts and use a router to make a $1/2$" x $1/2$" notch along the length of each cut. Again, these notches will support the table top. Attach each rail using two screws on each end (fig. c). The finished product should resemble the wooden frame of a house without a roof.

5. Place the plywood top onto the finished frame. Rest the 47" x 18" plywood in the notches you've prepared in the frame. Nail in place (fig. d).

And the best part is, you *never* have to use a coaster.

6. Staining and capping. Once the table is built, use wood putty to fill any exposed holes. Coat the whole sucker with your favorite wood stain. Once it dries, coat the surface of the table with a $1/8$" layer of epoxy. Arrange the caps on the epoxy in any pattern you like. After the epoxy dries, spread a light coating of polyurethane across the caps to protect them from rust. (In the table shown, we used Liquid Nails—see www.Liquidnails.com—to attach each individual cap.)

VARIATIONS

My dad was never content to just do the basics. As you can see in the table shown above, he added a few stylistic details—the notched edges of the end rails and, most notably, the rope poles. If you want to make similar rope poles, you just need two 15" lengths of sturdy steel pipe (1" in diameter), about 180" of sisal rope, a handful of nails, wood glue, and a propane torch. Before putting the end rails together, use a router to make 1.5" deep, $7/8$" diameter holes inside each of the 20" pieces. After you assemble the end rails, insert the pipe into these holes. Coat the pipe with liberal amounts of wood glue, then nail one end of the sisal rope to the wood support. Wrap it tightly around the length of the pipe, then nail the end down on the other side. For more texture and a more finished look, gently run a propane torch up and down the length of the roped pipe.

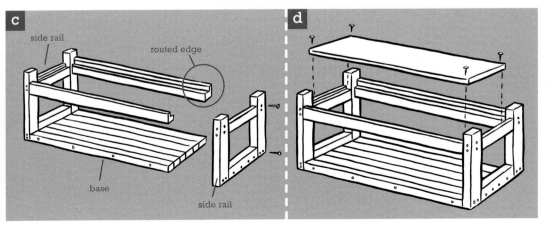

c

side rail

routed edge

base

side rail

d

From the National Register of Historic Beer Places.

THE BEER CAN HOUSE

Was John Milkovisch a true artistic visionary, or just a guy who really liked to drink cheap beer? Either way, his legendary Beer Can House at 222 Malone Street in Houston, Texas, remains a testament to what one man can do if he saves enough cans. Starting in 1949, Milkovisch, a railroad seat upholsterer, began cutting up aluminum beer cans and flattening them into rectangles. Then in 1966 he started tacking them on along the sides of his wood-frame bungalow, creating shimmering walls of metal. That was followed by chains made from the can tops and bottoms, which he draped from the roof. By the time Milkovisch died in 1988, he'd used an estimated 50,000 cans, painstakingly drained, cut, flattened, and affixed to his abode, which attracts scores of visitors every year and has been hailed as a "gem of folk creativity." When asked if he bought particular cans to form artistic effects, Milkovisch told an interviewer, "Sometimes I do. I buy what's on special."

For years the Beer Can House was laid bare to the elements—insects, hurricanes, vandals. But fortunately for Beer Can House enthusiasts everywhere, Houston's Orange Show Foundation purchased the home and started a costly restoration. If you'd like to build your own beer-can house, you should do two things: Clear it with your spouse, and start drinking now.

BEER-CAN AIRPLANE

Pilot D. P. Mathis was drinking beer with a couple of his buddies when one of them issued a challenge: Was it possible to make a plane using nothing but beer cans? And thus a new beer-can craft subgenre was born. Mathis's company, B. C. Air Originals, offers plans that will teach you how to create beer-can models of biplanes, helicopters, multiengine planes, or even planes that actually fly in the air. Mathis promises that you don't need any special tools—just a bunch of empties and some patience, as planes can take anywhere from 3 to 6 hours to assemble. Visit www.bcairoriginals.com to choose your dream plane.

BEER-CAN CREATURES

Talk about buzz: This elaborate insect was fashioned from a can of African beer. The anatomically correct shrimp was created out of a Heineken can. Try it at home! Or you can order your favorites at www.globalcrafts.org.

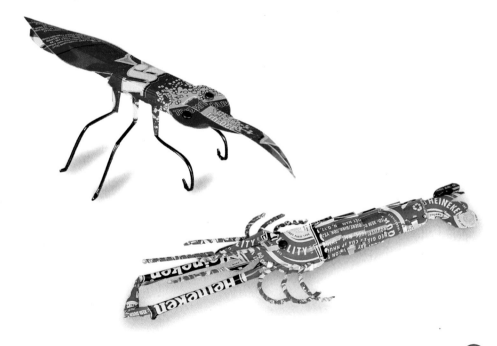

GAMES BEER DRINKERS PLAY

Beer is entertainment in itself, to be sure, but there's only so much fun to be had around discussing hops. This is why human beings invented beer games. Here are some of the best.

QUARTERS

EQUIPMENT: 2 to 8 people, lots of beer, a quarter, and a small tumbler or shot glass.

HOW TO PLAY: Take turns bouncing a quarter off the table, trying to make it land inside the tumbler. If you make it, you can order anyone at the table to drink, then you go again. If you miss, the next person takes a turn. Sink three quarters in a row, and you get to create a house rule, which all players must obey. The more creative and devious, the better. You might say, "Everyone must say proper names backward, or not at all." Or "Everyone must speak in Elvish." Anyone who fails to heed the rule must finish his or her beer.

HOW TO MAKE THIS MORE DEVIOUS: Have players pitch their quarters into a tumbler full of beer, and force everyone to drink from this glass. Make sure no one swallows the quarter.

BEERAMID

EQUIPMENT: 2 to 8 people, plenty of beer, and a deck of playing cards.

HOW TO PLAY: Build the "beeramid" (rhymes with "pyramid") with the playing cards. Lay out seven cards facedown, side by side. Overlap these cards with a row of six, then overlap them with a row of five, and so on. Distribute the remaining cards as evenly as possible among the players. The dealer turns over the first card in the bottom level, and the fun begins.

If you have the same card, you can force anyone to take a drink. If you don't have the same card, you can bluff and make someone else take a drink. However, that person may call your bluff by saying "bullshit." If you actually have the card, the person who accused you of bluffing must drink twice. If you were bluffing, you must drink twice. This continues to the next level, only now the penalty is two drinks. On the third level, it's three drinks, and so on, all the way to the top of the beeramid, where things get ugly real fast. Say you're on level five, and you accuse someone of bluffing. That person isn't bluffing. This means your sorry butt must take ten drinks. Life is tough at the top, isn't it?

HOW TO MAKE THIS MORE DEVIOUS: Anyone caught bluffing on the top level should be forced to drink a penalty beer—the cheapest, skunkiest, most evil-tasting brew the host can find.

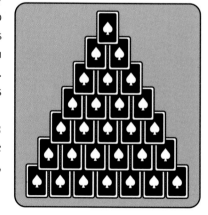

BEER CHESS

EQUIPMENT: This can get expensive but it's worth it. You'll need 64 square coasters (any kind will do, as long as the backs are blank) and 26 bottles and cans to use as playing pieces. To assemble the board, use the blank side of the coaster as a "white" space, and the decorated side as the "black" space. Arrange them in an 8 by 8 checkerboard pattern on any surface, ideally a dark wooden table.

	WHITE	BLACK
PAWNS	Bud Light (8 pony cans)	Budweiser (8 pony cans)
ROOKS	Miller Lite (2 12-oz. cans)	MGD (2 12-oz. cans)
KNIGHTS	Rolling Rock Light (2 12-oz. cans)	Rolling Rock (2 12-oz. cans)
BISHOPS	Coors Light (2 12-oz. cans)	Coors (2 12-oz. cans)
QUEEN	Michelob Light (1 bottle)	Michelob (1 bottle)
KING	Bud Light (1 bottle)	Budweiser (1 bottle)

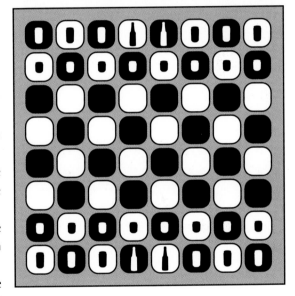

HOW TO PLAY: Follow the traditional rules, but with these extra penalties, just to keep things interesting:

1. When you move a piece, you must sip from it.
2. If your piece is captured, you must drink the entire piece.
3. Castling requires two sips: one from the king, one from the rook.
4. En passant requires only one sip (as in a standard pawn move).
5. When your pawn reaches the eighth rank and is exchanged for a queen (or other piece), your opponent must drink the remainder of the pawn.
6. Once you sip a piece, you must move that piece.
7. You can take as long as you want to drink a captured piece, but the piece must be quickly consumed if another of your pieces is captured.
8. If you are put in check, you must sip from the king.
9. Passing out constitutes a resignation.
10. If you are checkmated, you must drink the remaining beer in your king, the remaining beer in your opponent's king, and the remaining beer in all of your pieces.

HOW TO MAKE THIS MORE DEVIOUS: For the love of God, aren't you drunk enough already?

Other Popular Beer Amusements

SKITTLES

No, not the cloying fruit candies. Skittles is a traditional English pub game that resembles bowling—it involves nine pins—but it uses a roll of cheese instead of a ball. The game fell into decline after World War II, but some English pubs have been bringing it back, sometimes in smaller, table-sized versions.

DARTS

Why people enjoy combining alcohol with sharp objects that can easily puncture eyeballs is beyond me. But good luck finding a sports bar without at least one dartboard—they're ubiquitous. The game was created in the Middle Ages, when bored English soldiers took turns flinging arrows at a beer barrel cover. The soldier who aimed his arrows closest to the center—where there was a piece of cork—won the game. Darts made their way into bars in 1908, when an English pub owner named Anakin was taken to court for including a game of chance in his establishment; this was strictly forbidden under English law. But Anakin proved that darts were a game of skill, not chance, and in a stunning display of dart prowess, managed to perfectly hurl three darts into the "20" wedge. Anakin won his case; darts flourished.

If Ester makes this shot, poor Fred's in for a long night.

Bowling and beer—perfect together.

BOWLING

Why people enjoy combining alcohol with heavy marble balls that can easily crush a man's skull is beyond me. There's no historical data on this, but beer probably became popular with bowlers because there was pretty much nothing else to do while waiting for your turn, except watch other people bowl. Modern bowling lanes offer fancy black lights, special effects, and glow-in-the-dark pins, but I insist you still need a good draft pitcher to get through other people's frames.

KARAOKE

There are only two things on Earth that can make an otherwise intelligent, cultured person grab a microphone and start belting out "Afternoon Delight" in front of total strangers: a lot of beer, and a Karaoke song list. If you're ever forced to sing karaoke in front of your friends or coworkers, and you simply haven't had enough beer to drink, cheat and pick something by Elvis. Then ham it up. People will laugh and pay attention to your impression, not your vocal abilities.

BAR QUIZZES

These were (and still are, as of this writing) all the rage at the turn of this century. Pub quizzes go by many different names—Quizzo, Quizmaster, or even Bar Exams—but they all fit the same pattern: Teams of beer drinkers band together to answer a series of trivia questions posed by a quizmaster in an attempt to win cash, free food, or free beer. Don't make the mistake of thinking this is a light, breezy bar game. Teams are deadly serious about winning; pity the fool who doesn't know Indiana Jones's first name. (Answer: Henry.)

BEER AND THE APPLIED SCIENCES

"Not all chemicals are bad. Without chemicals such as hydrogen and

oxygen, for example, there would be no way to make water, a vital

ingredient in beer."—*Dave Barry*

Some of the most stunning scientific advances of the past 500 years owe thanks to beer. You won't hear any Nobel or Pulitzer Prize–winners admit this, but c'mon, do you really think somebody could have invented quantum mechanics without a couple of cold ones? In this section, science repays the debt. Take a spin through biology, physiology, chemistry, and higher math the way they were meant to be studied: through the eyes of beer.

HEALTH AND BEER

You have questions about beer and your body. We have answers.

Q: CAN MAN LIVE ON BEER ALONE?
A: YES, TECHNICALLY.

Conventional barroom wisdom claims that it's possible for human beings to sustain themselves on Guinness and milk. The argument goes that Guinness contains many of the essential vitamins and minerals, and milk supplies the required calcium and fat. Surprisingly, this is true, says Dr. Nigel Goodwin at the University of Nottingham, writing in *New Scientist* magazine, especially if you add a glass of orange juice for the vitamin C.

There's one catch: To receive your daily nutritional requirements, you'd have to drink 1 glass of orange juice, 2 glasses of milk, and 47 pints of Guinness.

Q: WHY DOES BEER GIVE YOU A BIG GUT?
A: THE JURY'S OUT ON THE WHOLE BEER BELLY THING—DON'T SEND YOUR FAVORITE BREW TO DEATH ROW JUST YET.

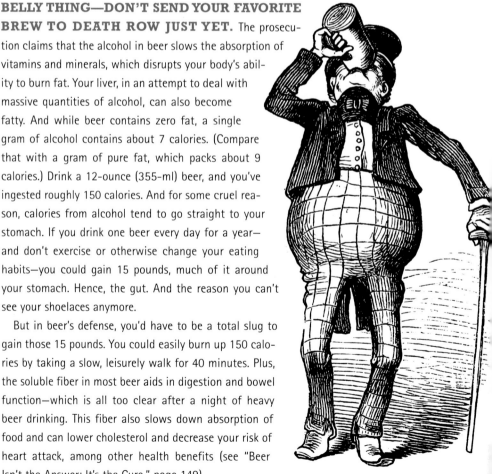

The prosecution claims that the alcohol in beer slows the absorption of vitamins and minerals, which disrupts your body's ability to burn fat. Your liver, in an attempt to deal with massive quantities of alcohol, can also become fatty. And while beer contains zero fat, a single gram of alcohol contains about 7 calories. (Compare that with a gram of pure fat, which packs about 9 calories.) Drink a 12-ounce (355-ml) beer, and you've ingested roughly 150 calories. And for some cruel reason, calories from alcohol tend to go straight to your stomach. If you drink one beer every day for a year—and don't exercise or otherwise change your eating habits—you could gain 15 pounds, much of it around your stomach. Hence, the gut. And the reason you can't see your shoelaces anymore.

But in beer's defense, you'd have to be a total slug to gain those 15 pounds. You could easily burn up 150 calories by taking a slow, leisurely walk for 40 minutes. Plus, the soluble fiber in most beer aids in digestion and bowel function—which is all too clear after a night of heavy beer drinking. This fiber also slows down absorption of food and can lower cholesterol and decrease your risk of heart attack, among other health benefits (see "Beer Isn't the Answer; It's the Cure," page 149).

Drink 12 ounces and call me in the morning: For a list of all the ailments beer can *really* cure, see page 149.

Q: WHY DOES BEER MAKE YOUR BREATH SMELL BAD?

A: ALCOHOL DRIES OUT YOUR MOUTH, which makes it easier for bacteria to thrive, which makes your mouth funkier than Morris Day and the Time. Making matters worse, you're getting it coming and going—alcohol leaves your body in a number of ways, including your breath. Despite this, many people hook up after consuming numerous pints of beer at the local sports bar. Go figure.

Q: WHY DO BEER DRINKERS TEND TO BURP A LOT?

A: BECAUSE BURPING THE ALPHABET ONLY SEEMS LIKE A GOOD

IDEA WHEN YOU'RE DRUNK. Also, beer is a carbonated beverage, which means it's packed with pressurized air—and if enough of this stuff gets trapped in your stomach, it's going to stage a jailbreak. But the biggest cause of burping is swallowing too much air. That can happen when you chew food or drink liquids. (And let's face it, if you're drinking beer, you're not taking slow, cautious, measured sips.) Air bubbles can get caught in your esophagus or in your stomach, but the result is the same either way.

Q: WHY DO DRUNK PEOPLE GET "BEER GOGGLES"?

A: IN 2002, PROFESSORS AT GLASGOW UNIVERSITY CREATED A STUDY TO DETERMINE WHY THE SO-CALLED "BEER GOGGLES" EFFECT OCCURS. Beer goggles, of course, are the invisible pieces of eyewear that mysteriously appear in front of your eyes when you drink too much, and through these lenses, even pimple-faced, slack-jawed, mouth-breathing geeks start to look like Jude Law.

Eighty students at Glasgow University volunteered for the study. Forty of them were given either two pints of lager or two and a half glasses of wine; the other half remained stone-cold sober. Next, the volunteers were shown 120 color photos of students of the opposite sex (ages 18 to 26, from another university) and were asked to play a little game of "Hot or Not." Ratings were assigned on a scale of one to seven; one meant "highly unattractive," while seven meant "highly attractive."

Surprise, surprise—the tipsy students were far more generous with their aesthetic appraisals of the student photos. Officially, the researchers discovered that men and women who have consumed even a moderate amount of booze found the faces of the opposite sex 25 percent more attractive than their sober counterparts.

But don't blame those imaginary beer goggles. Blame the part of your brain called the "nucleus accumbens," which determines facial attractiveness. Professor Barry Jones theorized that alcohol affects this part of the brain and temporarily suspends your otherwise good judgment. This judgment, by the way, is an evolutionary gift. "Attractiveness provides a very important signal of mate quality," Professor Jones says. "It shows you have good genes and a healthy body." Which is further proof that human beings have been drinking beer for a long, long time.

Q: WHY DO WOMEN SEEM TO GET DRUNK MORE QUICKLY THAN MEN?

A: IF THIS WEREN'T TRUE, THE HUMAN RACE NEVER WOULD HAVE STOOD A CHANCE. And it may have something to do with stomach enzymes. A doctor at Mount Sinai Hospital School of Medicine in New York City found that an enzyme called chi-alcohol dehydrogenase (chi-ADH) was nearly twice as effective at breaking down alcohol in men than in women. Other studies suggest that lower body weight and a higher proportion of body fat also make people more susceptible to booze; women tend to be lighter and—okay, how can I say this without my wife kicking my ass? More curvaceous? Built differently? You get the idea.

Interestingly, that same Mount Sinai study found that women could hold their own with men if they were drinking beer-for-beer. The chi-ADH advantage for men only kicked in when drinking stronger stuff—wine and whiskey. So ladies, if you ever want to challenge a man to a drinking contest, yank the brewskies out of the fridge.

Q: THERE'S AN OLD ADAGE, "BEER BEFORE LIQUOR, NEVER SICKER; LIQUOR BEFORE BEER, NEVER FEAR." IS THIS TRUE?

A: ABSOLUTELY. The human body absorbs the alcohol in beer (and other carbonated drinks) much faster than it absorbs the alcohol in mixed drinks. Once you have a few beers, your system is primed to absorb alcohol more quickly, and those mixed drinks you have later will hit you much harder.

Q: HOW DOES A BREATHALYZER WORK?

A: FIRST, YOU HAVE TO UNDERSTAND HOW ALCOHOL SHOWS UP IN YOUR BREATH. When you take a sip of beer, the alcohol is absorbed through your mouth, throat, stomach, and intestines, and eventually makes its way to your bloodstream. There, it does nothing—it isn't broken down, it isn't chemically transformed, nada. It stays put. Some travels through your blood and into your lungs, where it evaporates when you breathe. Boom. Alcohol in your breath.

Now, the amount of alcohol in your breath is directly proportional to the alcohol in your bloodstream. This is called the "partition ratio," and typically, it's 2,100 to 1; that is, 2,100 milliliters of exhaled air represents 1 milliliter of blood. So if it's possible to measure the alcohol in your exhaled air, it just takes a bit of simple math to determine how much alcohol is in your bloodstream. Or as my college buddy John Lenox used to say, "the amount of blood in my alcohol stream."

Q: WHY DOES CHEAP BEER GIVE YOU AN ESPECIALLY NASTY HANGOVER?

A: CHALK IT UP TO MISTREATED YEAST. Kindly, humane brewers give yeast the loving attention it needs: easily fermentable sugars and nutrients. But if you skimp on the ingredients, or ferment your beer warm, or pull some other kind of money-saving stunt, the yeast will create some nasty byproducts. The worst of these is fusel oil, an impure form of alcohol that is especially tough for your body to metabolize. Beer that's been sitting around too long can also wreak havoc with your body. Never surrender to the urge to finish off a dying soldier the morning after a party—stale beer has already started to oxidize, turning some of the alcohol into acetaldehyde, one of those evil little byproducts that give you a hangover.

Fusel oil. Acetaldehyde. Remember those names, especially when you're lying in bed wondering why your hair hurts so much.

Q: WHAT'S THE BEST WAY TO RECOVER FROM A HANGOVER?

A: IF YOU THINK YOU CAN STOMACH IT, TRY DOWNING A PEANUT BUTTER, BANANA, AND HONEY SANDWICH ON WHITE BREAD ALONG WITH A GLASS OF ORANGE JUICE. Seriously. Your big night of drinking has depleted some fairly important vitamins, and getting them back will ease the pain. Bananas pack a hearty dose of magnesium, which will help relax the blood vessels pounding in your head (bananas can also ease nausea). The fructose sugar from the honey will give you some much-needed energy, and the orange juice will replace your vitamin C.

You can also take a few preventative measures, like eating a meal before you start to drink. Having food in your stomach will slow down the absorption of alcohol and give your body a chance to process it more efficiently. And remember: Hangovers are partially caused by dehydration. The more water you can suck down before going to bed, the less likely it is you'll want to remove your skull with a pair of bolt cutters the next morning.

BEER ISN'T THE ANSWER; IT'S THE CURE

Here's a mere sampling of the many human ailments that can be prevented or cured with beer. And if beer can't cure it, it will at least take your mind off it.

AIDS

This is going to sound ridiculous, but bear with me. There's a biotech company, GlobeImmune, in Aurora, Colorado, working on a kind of beer that could vaccinate drinkers against HIV. GlobeImmune cofounder Alex Franzusoff added an HIV gene to brewer's yeast, then injected the mixture into mice. The result? The yeast prompted an amazing killer T cell response. Human trials for a beer-based AIDS vaccine are next, and, let's face it, drinking beer sure beats a series of injections. "A beer version would ensure full compliance from our volunteers," agrees Franzusoff.

BRITTLE BONES

According to a study at Creighton University, in Omaha, Nebraska, moderate alcohol consumption increases the chance that you'll have stronger bones when you're a senior citizen. The lead author of the study found that old folks with the highest bone density had consumed two to four beers or glasses of wine per week throughout their adult lives. Of course, this study doesn't take into account the bone injuries sustained from drinking too many beers.

CANCER

This is also going to sound ridiculous, but German scientists have been working on an anti-cancer beer. There's an antioxidant in hops called xanthohumol, and apparently it's been shown to halt the growth of tumor cells. According to European press reports, the scientists are working with a Bavarian brewery on a type of beer that would feature an abundance of these special cancer-busting antioxidants.

HEART DISEASE

Researcher Henk Hendriks at the Nutrition and Food Research Institute in Zeist, the Netherlands, conducted a study that showed men who drank a glass of beer with dinner every night enjoyed a 30 percent increase in vitamin B_6—a vitamin that helps protect the heart. By comparison, red wine and Dutch gin only boosted B_6 by 15 percent.

KIDNEY STONES

This one's for the guys: Stout, porter, or other hops-heavy beers can help prevent calcium deposits from forming in your kidneys. That's a good thing, since calcium deposits eventually turn into painful, jagged asteroids of pain called kidney stones. Researchers in Finland tracked 27,000 men and found that every glass of beer they drank daily reduced their risk of kidney stones by 40 percent. If it's too late, beer can also help you flush out that kidney stone. Your doc might suggest cranberry juice, but beer does the same thing—it dilates your sensitive tubing (the ureters) so the stone can exit your body as painlessly as possible.

SORE MUSCLES

You can take an ice-cold can of your favorite beer and use it as an ice pack—the metal can transmits the cold quickly. Just drape it in a light fabric before applying it directly to your skin. When your neck, head, or hamstring starts feeling better, pop open the ice pack and enjoy.

UPSET STOMACH

Carbonated beverages are great for settling your stomach. A can of 7-Up would work, but last time we checked, 7-Up didn't contain alcohol—and alcohol is a pain reliever. "I've never seen a true medical study supporting this," said Larry L. Alexander, MD, medical director of Central Florida Regional Hospital's emergency department, in *Men's Health* magazine, "but I have patients who tell me it works."

Apparently, pinecones promote longer life, too.

Long Life
BEER

what's better than Long Life?...

THE PHYSICS AND CHEMISTRY OF BEER

Don't know much about chemistry? Don't sweat it. Here's everything you *should* have learned in your high school science classes.

THE MIRACLE OF FERMENTATION

In this section we'll walk through the process of how a beer is born. Let's start with the basics. First you need some complex carbohydrates. For beer, your complex carbohydrate can be grain, which you then malt and boil into a mix called "the wort." Add some yeast enzymes, and a process called fermentation begins. The chemical equation for fermentation looks like this:

$$COMPLEX\ CARBOHYDRATES => 2(CH_3CH_2OH) + 2(CO_2)$$

Relax—this isn't as scary as it looks. The first part is simply the grain; the arrow represents the fermentation process, and the other crap is the chemical equation for beer. Pay close attention to the stuff inside the parentheses:

$$CH_3CH_2OH$$

That's the chemical symbol for ethanol (aka ethyl alcohol), the active ingredient in beer, wine and liquor. So just to recap: Once you add yeast to the wort, the result is:

$$ETHANOL\ (CH_3CH_2OH)\ PLUS\ CARBON\ DIOXIDE\ (CO_2).$$

Congrats—a beer is born. Now you just have to keep oxygen and stray yeasts away from your newborn; these can ruin its shelf life.

An important reminder: Ethyl alcohol is drinkable but methyl (wood) alcohol and isopropyl (rubbing) alcohol are not. Interestingly enough, ethanol can also be used as an industrial solvent, but since drinkable ethanol is taxed by the government, companies will add toxic chemicals to the ethanol to make it undrinkable, and therefore untaxable. This is called denatured ethanol. Do not drink this if someone offers it to you. Even mixed with cranberry juice.

But I digress. Back to the chemistry lesson.

There are other chemical byproducts of fermentation. The most important are congeners—various acids, aldehydes, esters, ketones, phenols, tannins, and other names you really don't have to remember. Congeners are key, though. These can add to the flavor and color of your favorite alcoholic beverage, or can ruin it. Too many nasty congeners in a shot of vodka, for instance, will result in a horrific hangover.

That said, fermentation is a perfectly natural process, and Mother Nature knows her limits. No matter how hard you try, she'll never let you ferment anything that is more than 14 percent ethanol. To create your own version of Wild Turkey on the rocks, you need to involve distillation—a time-consuming process that concentrates alcohol. I don't think it's worth the hassle. Anyone can ferment beer, but to distill, you need a permit from your friends at the Bureau of Alcohol, Tobacco, and Firearms (ATF).

BEER AND SKUNKING

Beer lovers know when their beloved beverage has gone bad. You can't see it, but you sure can taste and smell it. Conventional wisdom states that beer is like a vampire: if light hits it, things turn ugly. That's why many beer bottles are green or brown—they filter out light.

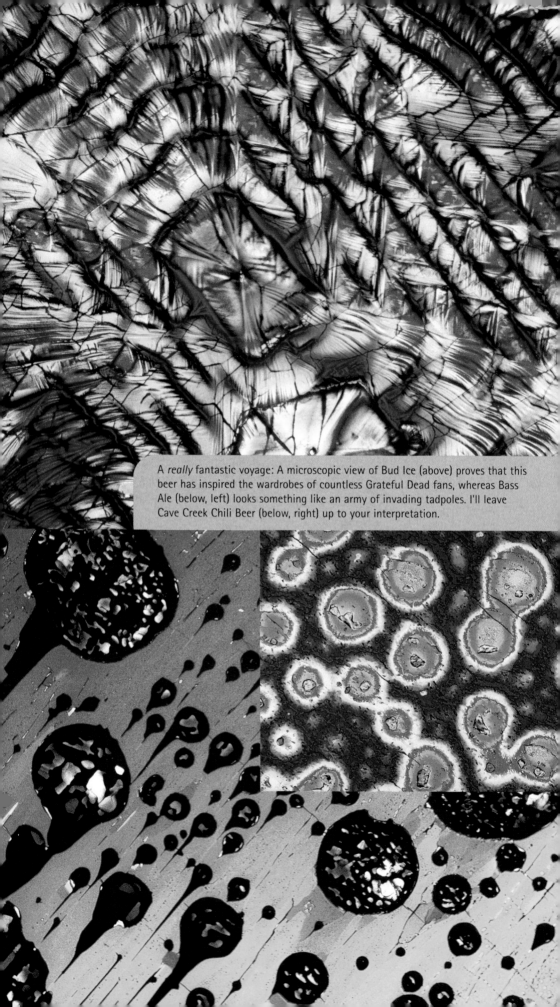

A *really* fantastic voyage: A microscopic view of Bud Ice (above) proves that this beer has inspired the wardrobes of countless Grateful Dead fans, whereas Bass Ale (below, left) looks something like an army of invading tadpoles. I'll leave Cave Creek Chili Beer (below, right) up to your interpretation.

A few years ago, researchers at the University of North Carolina came up with a computer simulation that shows exactly what happens when light hits certain molecules in hops. "The final product of the reaction turns out to be what we call 'skunky thiol,' an analogue of a compound found in skunk glands that produces a very bad taste and smell," study author Malcolm Forbes told *Scientific American*. That's right—on a molecular level, the word "skunky" turns out to be entirely accurate. And it takes just a few molecules of skunky thiol among the trillions of molecules in a bottle of beer to ruin the whole thing.

Brewers who want to stick by their clear bottles can use modified hops that will result in reactions with less of that skunky thiol, says Forbes.

BEER UP CLOSE AND PERSONAL

Ever wonder what beer looks like under the microscope? Never been *that* drunk? Well, Michael C. Davidson, a senior research engineer at Florida State University, has pondered that question, and, in fact, has devoted an entire Web site to his findings: www.micro.magnet.fsu.edu/beershots/index.html. Davidson and his crew use polarized light microscopy to capture brilliant, colorful, and somewhat trippy images of beer at its most elemental level.

You might note that a pint of Sam Adams is not usually colored like a rainbow. That's because Davidson is taking a fine mist of the beer, freezing it, then highlighting the crystalline patterns through a process that . . . well, frankly, I'm not sure I follow. But the results sure are spectacular, and can be purchased in poster form for your living room wall. (Beers from around the world have been frozen and photographed for your aesthetic enjoyment.) For more on the technical details, visit www.micro.magnet.fsu.edu/beershots/beerphotos.html.

WHERE BEER FOAM COMES FROM

Even 10-year-olds know a carbonated beverage (such as beer) will foam like crazy if you shake it. But why? Beer is usually carbonated with carbon dioxide (CO_2). When the can is closed, the pressure inside the can is higher than the pressure outside. Pop open the top, and there's a sudden pressure drop, which causes some of the CO_2 to bubble out of the beer, forming the familiar and comforting head. But if you shake the hell out of the can you're only increasing the pressure inside the can, which means the pressure drop will be all the more drastic. Hence, the beer will foam up and out and all over your pants.

A nice foam head is desirable because it's both aesthetically pleasing and an indication of beer freshness. A glass of beer is *supposed* to have a decent head, and beer brewers are careful to ensure a close-to-perfect head appears after every pour. Heineken, for instance, has a rule that a beer head should last five minutes. If a batch doesn't live up to this goal, it's rejected.

The way you pour a beer can influence the head, too. Beer from a keg almost always has a great head, because the beer is coming out so fast, and the pent-up carbon dioxide is being released like crazy. Beer foams in a glass because of microscopic imperfections in the glass itself. These tiny nicks trap gas bubbles, which eventually grow and rise to the surface. Your average glass of beer has a head of one million bubbles,

with the bubbles packed fifty to one hundred deep.

Eventually, the bubbles dry up and release their carbon dioxide, and the foam fades. Don't dig head? There's an old trick you can use to get rid of it—simply run your finger down the side of your nose, then stick it in your beer. Your facial grease breaks down the walls of the carbon dioxide bubbles quickly. Just don't go handing the beer to a friend.

WHAT WOULD BEER BE LIKE IN SPACE?

Beer as we know it depends on Earth's gravity—the carbon dioxide tries to escape it, while the beer itself is contained by it. But one reader of *New Scientist* magazine posed an interesting question: What would happen if an astronaut in orbit tried to enjoy a cold one? Would there be a head? Would the beer float around everywhere?

One scientist from California, Todd Dark-Fox, said that it depended on the container. Beer released from a glass would just float out in globs. But if you popped open a beer can, the microgravity effects would cause the beer to shoot out and cover the nearest instrument panel. Bubbles would still form, but not in the way we're used to—at the top of the beer. Instead, the bubbles would remain inside the beer, making it look like a cup of something a freshman pumped out of the keg.

It's probably a good thing beer wouldn't work in space—human beings need gravity to burp up excess gas. The carbonation in even a pony bottle of Bud would wreak havoc on an astronaut's internal organs; because of this, astronauts aren't allowed carbonated beverages in space. You didn't think they picked Tang because of the taste, did you?

Houston, we do *not* have a problem.

THE PHYSICS OF BEER-CAN WIDGETS

In an attempt to duplicate the frothy head of a draft beer in canned beer, some brewers have come up with devices called "widgets." (You can tell a beer has a widget if it sounds like a spray paint can when you shake it—gently!) The idea is that when you pour out the beer, the widget works its magic and gives you a nice fat head on your brew. But how does it work?

The widget, usually a plastic device, contains nitrogen and a tiny valve. The brewer puts the widget at the bottom of the can, then pours in the beer. A small amount of nitrogen is pumped into the header space, found between the top of the beer and the can. Next, the beer is pasteurized; the heat from that process enlarges the widget and increases the pressure in the can. The beer is shipped. You purchase it. When you pop open the can, pressure is released; this opens that tiny valve in the widget. The nitrogen is released, creating small bubbles that are white and long lasting—instant head.

The results are mixed; some people think that beer-can widgets work wonders, while others think it's all a marketing ploy. You can decide for yourself by picking up a can of Guinness, Murphy's Stout, Beamish, or other brands.

How to Crush a Beer Can

BEGINNER'S METHOD

This is the only reliable way to crush the living hell out of a can with minimum risk to your body. Place the can on a sturdy floor, preferably a concrete patio. Now stomp your strongest foot directly on the top of the can. This is where skill and practice are needed. If you're off the true center even by a hair, the can will simply bend in half, or worse, skitter free across the concrete. But if you nail it just right, the sides of the can will have no choice but to completely and utterly collapse, not unlike the Backstreet Boys' careers. The sides are designed to withstand a certain amount of internal pressure, not the aerial assault you unleash from above. The top and bottom of the can will meet, forming an aluminum sandwich. Flip it away, and have another beer.

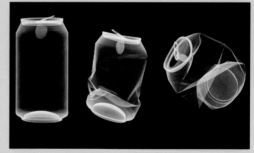

ADVANCED METHOD

Fill a saucepan with cold water. Pour a tablespoon of water into the empty can. Using a pair of kitchen tongs, hold the can over an open flame to boil the water. (You'll know it's boiling when vapor starts emerging from the top.) Let the water boil for 30 seconds, then quickly invert the can and dip it into the saucepan. The can will collapse almost instantaneously.

How does this cool trick work? When you heat the can, the vapor from the boiling water pushes the air out of the can, leaving nothing but water vapor. Dunking the can into cold water causes the vapor to condense, leaving the can empty. And when the can is empty, the pressure of the air outside crushes it.

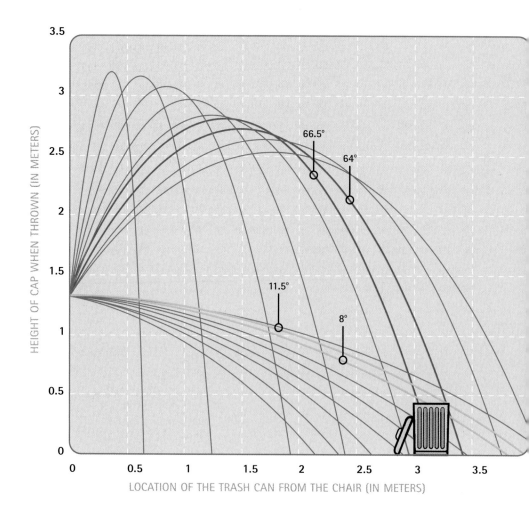

HEIGHT OF CAP WHEN THROWN (IN METERS)

LOCATION OF THE TRASH CAN FROM THE CHAIR (IN METERS)

THE PHYSICS OF A FLYING BEER BOTTLE CAP

There are many things you can do with a bottle cap. Flip it around your fingers like a coin. Flip it in the air. But perhaps the most important thing you can do is to flip it into the nearest trash container. This is not as easy as it sounds—especially if you don't feel like getting out of your chair and walking to the trash can.

I asked Dr. J. R. White, professor of nuclear engineering at the University of Massachusetts in Lowell, to determine the exact angle to use when pitching bottle caps into the trash can. He conducted a series of physics experiments to find the answer. The official title for the resulting paper was "Plotting Object Trajectories for Simple 2-D Motion Assuming Only a Gravity Force in the Y-Direction," but I prefer to call this experiment "Operation Cap Chuck."

According to Doc White, the optimal conditions are as follows:

- The vertical position of the cap with you sitting with arm extended should be about 4 feet (1.2 m) above the floor.
- The location of the front edge of the trash can should be about 10 feet (3 m) from where you are sitting.
- The trash can should be about 1.5 feet (0.45 m) high with a width of about 1 foot (0.3 m).
- A reasonable initial speed for tossing the cap is about 20 to 30 feet (6 to 10 m) per second.

Now he sets us up with the problem: "The initial angle has to be such that the x-directed velocity is positive, which gives a range of $-\pi/2 < \theta < \pi/2$. This is the maximum range possible and our goal will be to determine the values of θ that lead to success."

I'll admit, he loses me a bit here. But I think he's saying that he's trying to find the values of θ—the proper angle—that will land the beer bottle cap in the trash.

To support his argument, he provided two pages of parameters and graphs and "dot arithmetic" and other stuff I really can't follow. I'm sorry to say it, but I absolutely sucked at physics, even though I somehow landed in the Advanced Placement class in high school. What makes this even more embarrassing is that Doc White says that this whole experiment is extremely rudimentary; any sub-par physics major at a community college should be able to duplicate it. Gee. Thanks.

Conclusion: There are two possibilities for success. Either you try to pitch that cap at an angle between 8 and 11.5 degrees from the horizontal, which will guarantee one successful trajectory, or try for an angle between 64 and 66.5 degrees.

Or, if you're like me and miserable at physics, just haul your ass out of your chair and go for the sure thing.

ALTERNATE SCIENTIFIC APPLICATIONS FOR BEER

Does your non-beer-loving significant other give you the fisheye while you lug in a case of your favorite beer? Stop 'em dead in their tracks with this astounding array of alternate scientific applications for beer. You can actually save a life, beautify your home and garden, and enjoy a head full of shiny, lustrous hair with a single can of beer. Even the cheap stuff.

SCIENTIFIC APPLICATION #1: FIREFIGHTING

You're caught in the kitchen with a pan full of flames that used to be a pan full of dinner. You don't have a fire extinguisher handy. No sweat. Open the fridge, grab a can or bottle of beer, shake it up a few times, and unleash the spray on the fire. Beer is mostly water, and the short, pressurized burst will help tame the flames. (And don't worry—there's not enough alcohol in the beer to do more damage.) Just make sure you don't use it on a grease fire, though, or that pressurized burst will send the flames all over the kitchen and won't extinguish anything. You might even keep a can or two handy where fires tend to break out—near your backyard grill or your car, for instance.

SCIENTIFIC APPLICATION #2: PERSONAL HYGIENE

Everybody's heard that beer can double as shampoo and conditioner. This is true, but don't pour it straight from the bottle over your long, flowing locks—the alcohol will dry your hair up faster than Justin Guarini's recording career. Instead, pour a cup into a saucepan, boil it (which will burn away the alcohol), and let it cool, then mix it with some of your favorite shampoo. The result will be shiny, thinker, lustrous hair—thanks to the protein in the beer—and an excuse to keep beer in the shower.

You can also use beer as an emergency hair-styling product. If you have a cowlick that's acting up, just wet your fingers with some beer and smooth things back into place. Beer is sticky enough to hold your hair where you want it—at least until you've had more beer and no longer care what your hair looks like.

SCIENTIFIC APPLICATION #3: RUST BUSTING

Carbonated beverages—basically, liquid with pressurized air—can help break up rust, and just might give you the edge you need to finally turn that stubborn bolt on the side of your mother-in-law's head.

SCIENTIFIC APPLICATION #4: METAL CLEANSING

Greg Smith, the general manager of the Idaho Brewing Company, swears by using beer to clean the copper-topped tables in his Idaho Falls brewpub. "Because of its acidity," he told *Men's Health* magazine, "you can just pour some on, let it sit for a while, then wipe it off. It also works well on Revere Ware pots."

'Shampoo & Set' SENSATION!

AUTHENTIC UNRETOUCHED PHOTOGRAPHS
※ TAKEN IN THE PRESENCE OF A COMMISSIONER FOR OATHS

PROVE THAT IN 9 MINUTES
Linc·o·Lin Beer Shampoo
GIVES FINE HAIR 'BODY'!

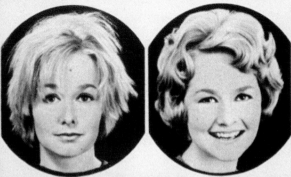

1. SHE SHAMPOO'D AND RINSED with LINC-O-LIN BEER SHAMPOO

She had no skilled professional help, no hairdresser was even present.

2. TIME BETWEEN PHOTOS—90 MINS.

—during which she dried and set her own hair absolutely unaided and using no other dressing or finish.

3. ABSOLUTELY AUTHENTIC *

A Commissioner for Oaths was present to witness the whole operation and the resulting photographs are entirely unretouched.

This is undoubtedly the most sensational Shampoo advertisement ever published! It was possible only because Linc-O-Lin Beer 'Shampoo and Set' positively **DOES** give even fine and difficult hair **'BODY'**—and now we've dared to **PROVE IT!**

Try marvellous Linc-O-Lin Shampoo yourself and see what its ready built-in Beer Rinse and Set can do for your hair! From chemists in Sachets or Baby Barrels.

Linc·o·Lin Beer Shampoo

SCIENTIFIC APPLICATION #5: PEST REMOVAL

According to the University of Illinois's *Home, Yard & Garden Pest Newsletter*, you can use beer to draw snails and slugs away from your prized flowers and plants and into a devious trap. All you have to do is pour a can of cheap beer—you don't want to break out a bottle of top-fermenting Duvel for this one—into a wide-mouthed jar or shallow pan. Now, sink the jar or pan into the middle of your lawn, away from your expensive flora. Snails and slugs will be attracted to the yeasty smell of the beer, crawl into the bar, and drown.

SCIENTIFIC APPLICATION #6: LAWN CARE

Plants enjoy an occasional good brew—the fermented sugars can give grass energy to grow. When choosing a beer for your lawn, go for one without preserving chemicals, such as home brew, Rolling Rock, and many microbrews. (Check the label to be sure.)

Do Plastic Six-Pack Rings Really Kill Dolphins and Seabirds?

The short answer: Yes, they do. But it's not like it's an epidemic. The six-pack ring thing has been blown out of proportion by well-meaning environmentalists, who unfairly taint our favorite beer-can containment device with the blood of innocent animals.

Six-pack rings earned a stigma thanks to the 1990 book, *50 Simple Things You Can Do to Save the Earth*. Simple Thing #2: Cut up those plastic rings, otherwise poor seabirds and dolphins and other marine life will entangle their beaks and snouts in them and die. An Associated Press story claimed that one million seabirds and 100,000 marine mammals were killed by six-pack rings (and other forms of plastic trash) every year. By the early 1990s, frat boys everywhere were doing their part by snipping each loop of their six-pack rings before tossing them idly onto the back lawn.

The truth is, discarded fishing gear—monofilament fishing line, hooks, lures, nets—is the biggest marine animal killer. The Center for Marine Conversation tracked 1,089 instances of animal entanglement between 1989 and 1998, and only 7 percent were caused by six-pack rings. Fishing gear accounted for a staggering 42 percent. But do tree-huggers pick on fisherman? Nope. They go after the beer drinkers.

Today's six-pack rings are designed to disintegrate in the sunlight within weeks. Sure, you can slice up those rings just to be safe, but it's really only a problem if you routinely discard your beer refuse on beaches or near bodies of water. (If you're pitching it in the trash, that six-pack ring will likely find its way to a landfill, far from the innocent snout of a blue dolphin.) Then again, if you're dating or married to an environmentalist, snipping the rings is probably an easy way to earn points, so go ahead. Knock yourself out.

BEER MATH

Whether you're having a sip, a six-pack, or a truckload, it's handy to know the measures of beer used around the world.

2 OUNCES = 1 SHOT

2 SHOTS = 1 PONY
+ 1 OUNCE

2 PONIES = 1 MIDDY

1 SHOT = 1 BUTCHER
+ 1 PONY   OR 1 SEVEN

1 OUNCE + 1 SHOT = 1 PINT
+ 1 MIDDY   (US)

2 SHOTS = 1 PINT
+ 1 PINT (US)   (UK)

20 PINTS (US) = 1 CASE

3 CASES + 4 PINTS (US) = 1 PONY KEG

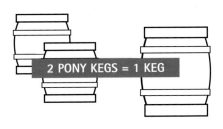

2 PONY KEGS = 1 KEG

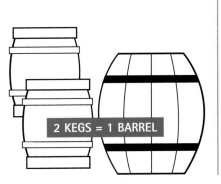

2 KEGS = 1 BARREL

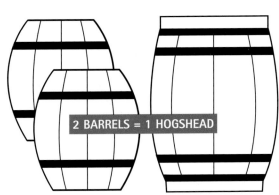

2 BARRELS = 1 HOGSHEAD

BEER AND THE ARTS

"There was no beer on the island, man. If they had beer they would have had, like, big-ass orgies." —*Joshua Leonard reflecting on "Gilligan's Island" in* The Blair Witch Project

Some misguided people accuse beer drinkers of being ignorant, incapable of appreciating the finer arts. They believe that a beer lover's knowledge of literature goes no further than burping the letters of the alphabet, that music appreciation goes no further than the second verse of "Louie, Louie." Boy, are those people are wrong! The world of beer has long embraced and enriched the fields of design, painting, cinema, television, literature, and possibly even interpretative dance. Want proof? Just turn the page, and prepare to feast your eyes and ears.

"Here's one I can understand!"

This man may not be an art expert, but he *knows* fine beer when he tastes it. There are millions of people like him . . . people who like the *taste* of Schlitz so much that no other beer is in the picture for them.

**Schlitz tastes so good to so many people,
it's the first in sales in the U.S.A.**

RADIO HEADLINER: "The Halls of Ivy", with the Ronald Colmans, Wednesdays, NBC
TELEVISION HIT: "Schlitz Playhouse of Stars", Fridays, CBS-TV

The Beer that made Milwaukee Famous

Exhibit A: "Here's one I can understand!" I couldn't have said it better myself.

THE METROPOLITAN GALLERY OF BEER ART

Beer advertisements are like movie posters and book covers: sometimes, they have absolutely nothing to do with the product being advertised. The world of the beer advertisement is a world of hyper-reality, where colors are brighter, the mountains are taller, the fauna is fuller, the air is cleaner and the foamy head on top of a pilsner glass is everlasting. Beer advertisements exist in an alternate universe, a surreal place where tilting bottles of Corona take the place of the Leaning Tower of Pisa; where Japanese royalty sit around worshipping a cold bottle of Asahi; where gorgeous models actually stop to hang out with ordinary beer-slurping schmoes; where Billy Dee Williams will help you get laid.

What does all of this have to do with the beer inside the bottle? Pretty much nothing. But like most advertising art, the beer ad exists to evoke a mood. Breweries hope it's the "Gee, I ought to go buy a six-pack" kind of mood. Consider Exhibit A—the vintage Schlitz advertisement shown on the opposite page. Created in 1952 by artist John Falter, this painting of a painting appeals to the unique aesthetic of Joe Six Pack. "This man may not be an art expert," the ad copy reads, "but he *knows* fine beer when he tastes it. There are millions of people like him." And there were millions, indeed. Thanks in part to ingenious advertisements like this one, Schlitz ranked as one of the biggest brands in the United States during the 1950s.

Over the next few pages, we'll look at other examples of beer art. If at any point you don't stop and think, "Gee, I ought to go buy a six pack," you might want to stop and check your pulse.

Exhibit B

Beer Can Library, (1997) by Philadephia-based artist Virgil Marti. The cans represent the vast collection that Marti and his father collected years ago when Marti was growing up near St. Louis, Missouri. "I try to find beauty in those things I've been told aren't beautiful anymore," Mr. Marti explained to the Philadelphia *City Paper*. He also admitted that he wanted to make an ironic comment on "yuppies who thought microbrews were the new wine." If you're lucky enough to see *Beer Can Library* at an exhibit someday, just don't try to pluck a cold one from the shelf—it's wallpaper. (Turn the page to see the entire piece.)

La *Victoria* de México.

Exhibit C: Further masterpieces that blur the line between art and advertisement.

Wᴹ YOUNGER'S SPARKLING BITTER

Clear to the last dro...

3 of the best — McEWAN'S

Miller THE BEST MILWAUKEE

BOCK BE...

CARLSBERG BRYGGERIER

PORTER · PALE ALE

CARLSBERG BEER · CERVEZA DANEZA

J.C. JACOBSEN · KJØBENHAVN.

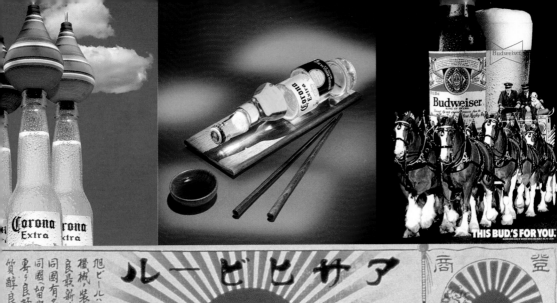

ASAHI BEER
OSAKA BEER BREWING CO. SUITA-MURA

THE ART OF THE BEER LABEL

ANIMALS

1. Mickey's Malt Liquor (U.S.): If there ever were a mascot to fit the hangover, this angry-looking hornet is it.

2. Foster's (Australia): A red kangaroo with its back to five stars—and suspiciously, no joey.

3. Mississippi Mud Black & Tan (U.S.): A gator with its jaws slightly open, just waiting for you to drink one too many of these bad boys and fall asleep in the swamp.

4. Löwenbräu (Germany): A lion with a tongue like Gene Simmons. The lion makes sense—Löwenbräu is German for "lion's brew." But what's the deal with that tongue?

5. Lion Lager (Sri Lanka). This lion strikes the same pose as the Löwenbräu lion, but doesn't look nearly as menacing.

6. Yuengling Lager (U.S.): A bald eagle fiercely guards a barrel of beer—presumably Yuengling. Thank God they're not endangered anymore.

7. Golden Eagle Lager Beer (India). Maybe it's me, but doesn't this alleged "eagle" look more like a Thanksgiving turkey?

8. Dinkel Acker CD Pils (Germany): These horses are on their way to deliver barrels of beer. Let's not get in their way.

9. Tecate (Mexico). Another bird, but this is one is draped in shadow and mystery—much like Mexico itself.

10. Dojlidy Zubr Beer (Poland). The Zubr mascot is a European Bison, but it also looks like something that will appear if you play with a Ouija board too much.

11. Hasserorder Premium Pils (Germany). This label features a small bird—pheasant? quail?—that actually could be roasted and served with the beer it's hawking. (Sorry.)

FANCIFUL CREATURES

12. Kirin Ichiban (Japan): A mythical beast that is half dragon. I'd like to see deer hunters take on this sucker.

13. Singha (Thailand): An ornate dragonlike creature.

14. Victory HopDevil (U.S.): A pleasant-looking demon with a face created from hop leaves. Don't call an exorcist—just enjoy this excellent beer.

15. Hobgoblin (U.K.). You know you've had too many when that thing on the label starts to look like Clark Gable.

HISTORICAL FIGURES

16. Samuel Adams Boston Lager (U.S.): Named, of course, for the great American patriot and brewer Samuel Adams. I always liked that the label bestows these two titles upon Mr. Adams, and that "brewer" always comes before "patriot."

17. Piast Beer (Poland): Named after legendary King Piast, who was to Poland what Arthur was to England.

18. Shakespeare Stout (U.S.): Many of Shakespeare's characters loved to drink beer, so it only seems appropriate to honor the Bard with a brew of his own.

13 **SINGHA**
FL. OZ.   MALT LIQUOR
BOON RAWD BREWERY CO., LTD.
BANGKOK, THAILAND

12 **KIRIN ICHIBAN**
一番搾り

15 **HOBGOBLIN**
16.9 fl.

18 **ROGUE**
SHAKESPEARE STOUT
1 PT. 6 FL. OZ.

14 **VICTORY Hop Devil** ALE PA

20 ST. SEBAS

17 1241 LESZEK · CZARNY 1288
Piast
Brewed and bottled
Wrocław
Premium   Be

19 OLD RASPUTIN
RUSSIAN IMPERIAL STOUT

21 **GREAT LAKES**
BREWING CO.
Eliot Ness
A Handcrafted Vienna-Styled Lager
from Cleveland, Ohio
12 fl. oz.

16 THE BOSTON BEER COMPANY
AMERICA'S
WORLD-CLASS BEER™
SAMUEL ADAMS
BOSTON LAGER®

Bayerischen Reinheits-
entsprechend gebrautes

**Aecht
Schlenkerla
Rauchbier**

<ges. gesch.>

WEIZEN

BREREI HELLER
BAMBERG

t. 09 FL. OZ.

25

**IRON CITY
BEER**

Premium Beer

Celebrating
a tradition of
brewing excellence
since 1861

140th Year
PITTSBURGH, PA

27

Köstritzer

Schwarzbier

Germany's Black
Lager

CONT. 12 FL. OZ.

24

SAPPORO
Imported

ORIGINAL DRAFT BEER

29

ed Stripe

JAMAICAN

BREWED & BOTTLED IN GERMANY

ST. PAULI GIRL

ST. PAULI BRAUEREI
BREMEN, GERMANY

1 Pint 8 FL. OZ.
710 ml

1 Pint 8 FL. OZ.
710 ml

BIER · BEER

26

22

CARIB

Carib

Lager

28

DRINK

NUDE

PEEL

MFG'D AND BOTTLED
FOR: NUDE BEER BY
COAST RANGE BREWERY,
GILROY, CA.

www.drinknudebeer.com

NUDE BEER

www.drinknudebeer.com

23

19. North Coast Old Rasputin Russian Imperial Stout (U.S.): Grigory Rasputin, aka, The Mad Monk of Imperialist Russia. Rasputin is noted for two things: surviving multiple attempts on his life and his creepy-ass beard.

20. St. Sebastiaan (Belgium). According to legend, the Catholic St. Sebastiaan was pierced by arrows but miraculously survived his wounds; on this label, ol' Sabby appears to be taking more of his "medication" to ease the pain.

21. Eliot Ness (U.S.): Named for the crime fighter who went head-to-head with Al Capone. Ness became Director of Public Safety in Cleveland, Ohio, where this beer is brewed.

Subliminal Messages

Is Rolling Rock trying to tell us something? The mysterious number "33" appears on every bottle, but the Latrobe Brewing Co. refuses to explain why. Numerous conspiracy theories abound. One has it that "33" refers to "1933," the year the Volstead Act was repealed, Prohibition went bye-bye, and Latrobe dusted off the vats and went back into business.

Another theory has it that "33" represents the number of words on the back of the painted bottle, as well as the number of letters in the ingredients list. A more plausible theory comes from StraightDope.com, which tracked down a former Latrobe CEO, who revealed that the "33" was nothing more than a printer's error—before the mistake could be caught, it had already made its way onto thousands of bottles. My personal theory? Latrobe put that number on the bottle to screw with the minds of thousands of beer drinkers.

DAMES

22. St. Pauli Girl (Germany): In recent years, the St. Pauli Girl's reputation has been sullied by a series of lowbrow ads that make a joke about "having your first girl." The lady deserves better than this, fellas.

23. Nude Beer (U.S.) Every bottle features a peel-off label that conceals a photograph of a naked woman. No word yet on whether the brewery plans to distribute "guy bottles" for Ladies' Night.

ORNATE

24. Köstritzer Schwarzbief (Germany): The emblems on the label date back to the 1500s and 1600s, and belong to the two castles in Thuringia, Germany, where the beer was originally brewed.

25. Aecht Schlenkerla Rauchbier Weizen (Germany): The beer tastes like somebody left a piece of bacon in a mug of porter, but the faux-parchment label is fantastic.

MINIMALIST

26. Red Stripe (Jamaica): Just red and white.

27. Iron City (U.S.): Just red, white, and black.

28. Carib Lager (West Indies): Just yellow, white, and . . . oooh! Blue!

29. Sapporo (Japan): Just silver and black. The Terminator of beer cans.

EXISTENTIAL

30. Birra Moretti (Italy): An older man in a hunter green suit closes his eyes and sips from a full mug of golden beer. Who is this man? Is he a government assassin? A businessman at the end of his rope? Why doesn't he look at his beer? Are the harsh realities of job starting to eat away at his soul? The best beer labels are ones that hint at a larger drama.

HUMOROUS

31. He'brew Genesis Ale (U.S.): The back label reads: "Exile Never Tasted So Good." Of course, this beer is kosher.

32. Three Stooges Beer (U.S.): Nyuk! Nyuk! Nyuk! Look at the souse! Look at the souse! Do we drink 'em? And how!

No Cash Redemption Value

According to college legend, if you can peel a label off a beer bottle without ripping or otherwise damaging it, that label can be redeemed for sex. Does it work? Let's put it this way: I still have a dozen of these things tucked away in my old college notebooks.

BEER COMMERCIALS AND SPOKESPERSONS

If you want to promote your beer, you have three basic options: 1) Hire a tough guy or former athlete; 2) hire an attractive woman, 3) hire someone to draw cute talking animals. Some of beer's best-known pitchmen have belonged to one of these three categories.

CARLING'S BLACK LABEL "MABEL"

Mabel was a hardworking and attractive bartender who responded with nothing but a smile and a wink to any doofus who yelled, "Hey, Mabel, Black Label!" The campaign was created by Lang, Fisher, and Stashower in 1951 and starred Jean Goodspeed, a New York City–based actress and model. The ads were so successful, other breweries started to parody them. One Labatt's TV spot featured a woman in dark sunglasses and a scarf over her head, sneaking out of a bar with a package under her arm. When a "man on the street" asks what she has in the package, she reluctantly reveals a six-pack of Labatt's. "Would you tell us your name?" the interviewer asks. The woman, knowing the ruse is over, removes her sunglasses. "Why,

yes. I'm Mabel." Of course, Labatt's didn't hire Jean Goodspeed—they simply found an attractive blonde who looked like her. The real Goodspeed retired in the mid-1950s to start a family, and Mabel became an animated cartoon character. The brewery hired a new Mabel in 1970, but she never caught on the way Goodspeed (or her animated doppelgänger) did. Mabel hung up her apron for good shortly thereafter.

THE HAMM'S BEAR

Theodore Hamm Brewing Company's first animal mascots were a bunch of beavers who played tom-tom drums. They didn't quite set the world on fire, so in 1952 Hamm introduced a cute animated bear with a serious beer gut. The commercials used a blend of live action nature footage along with its perpetually happy, bouncing, dancing Hamm's Bear. "Yes, from the land of sky blue waters, to you comes Hamm's, the beer as refreshing as the crisp, cool land it's brewed in. The beer that captures for you the wonderful refreshment of this enchanted Northland," the narrator said. The prancing bear never spoke, save for one spot in the mid-1960s when he said, "It bears repeating."

MISS RHEINGOLD

The most famous election in 1960 didn't have anything to do with John F. Kennedy or Richard Nixon. Instead, 22 million Americans eagerly cast their ballots to vote for the new Miss

RHEINGOLD ELECTION EXTRA!

Meet the six lovely candidates for

Miss Rheingold
1958

Read how you profit from the greatest beer promotion ever!

Long before *American Idol*, gorgeous women every-where competed for the title of Miss Rheingold.

Rheingold, a beer-ly tradition that began in 1942. Each year, hundreds of women—all of them registered models—would gather at the Waldorf-Astoria Hotel in New York City for preliminary judging. The field was narrowed to 13 women, whose faces would adorn ballots and beer cans throughout the New York area and New England. The winning Miss Rheingold would receive up to $50,000 in cash, plus other associated perks—a travel and wardrobe expense account, and of course, her visage plastered over millions of cans of Rheingold. Sometimes, even being a contestant was enough to kick-start a career. Tippi Hedren was a 1953 finalist and later starred in Alfred Hitchcock's *The Birds*.

Get your own damn beer: Today's Miss Rheingold is more confident and self-assured than her predecessors.

The last Miss Rheingold to win by popular vote was Celeste Yarnall in 1964; the next year, the brewer selected their own winner. What happened? Beer writer Will Anderson theorizes that while Miss Rheingold was always a white girl, Rheingold's consumer base was becoming increasingly African-American and Hispanic. So, the brewery opted to kill the campaign rather than alienate any consumers; Rheingold itself went out of business in 1976.

But nearly 40 years later, both the beer and the Miss returned. The newly revived Rheingold Brewing Co. launched an updated version of the contest, in which New York City–area female bartenders competed for the title.

THE PIELS: BERT AND HARRY

Long before Bartels and Jaymes, we had Bert and Harry Piel, the fictitious owners of the Piel Bros. Brewery Company in Brooklyn. Bert was

the short, cranky loudmouth, and his easygoing brother Harry was forever trying to calm Bert down after their carefully planned commercials went haywire. Bert and Harry (whose voices were provided by the comedy team of Bob Elliot and Ray Goulding) were far more popular than the beer they were created to promote. Thousands of letters to the imaginary brothers were sent to Piels headquarters in Brooklyn, and at its height, there were more than 100,000 members of the Bert and Harry Fan Club. The Piel Brothers "retired" in 1960, but a mock election in 1962 brought them back for a few more years.

THE MILLER LITE CAMPAIGN

Miller Lite's famous TV spots from the 1970s and 1980s lasted longer than even the most successful sitcoms. Their pitchmen were legion: Dick Butkus, John Madden, Bubba Smith, and Mickey Spillane, among dozens of other tough guys, all gathering to argue the merits of whether Lite tasted great or was less filling. McCann-Erickson came up with that timeless slogan, and it was originally conceived as a way to get burly, macho beer drinkers to be calorie-conscious without admitting it. ("Fewer calories" would imply a diet drink; "less filling" means you have room for more beer.) The campaign was a stunning success—Miller went from shipping 7 million barrels of Lite in 1973 to 31 million barrels in 1978. And the slogan survives today. In January 2003, Miller introduced a more controversial version of the ad, featuring two attractive, professional women debating the question of "Tastes Great or Less Filling?" The argument spirals out of control and somehow devolves into a wet T-shirt/mud wrestling contest.

Hamming it up: Deacon Jones and John Madden make lite beer seem macho.

THE SCHLITZ MALT LIQUOR BULL

Open a can of Schlitz Malt Liquor, then duck. According to popular ads of the late 1970s, upon popping the top, a huge black longhorn Brahma bull would charge out of the can, destroying every wall and window in sight. "If you don't have Schlitz, you don't have gusto," went the tagline. "Brother, you don't have beer." But in reality, the Schlitz bull was a 2,000-pound (907 kg) pussycat. His name was Zane, and he was neutered at birth by his owner, Ralph Helfer, who founded an animal behavioral center near Los Angeles.

If You've Got the Time . . .
. . . We've Got the Beer, and the Quiz

CAN YOU MATCH THE BEER TO ITS FAMOUS AD SLOGAN?

1. Tastes Great, Less Filling
2. Australian for Beee-ah
3. Why Ask Why?
4. The Beer That Made Milwaukee Famous
5. It's the Water!
6. Brewed with Pure Rocky Mountain Spring Water
7. From the Land of Sky Blue Waters to You, Comes . . .
8. For All You Do, This _____'s for You
9. Uncle Jackson's Watching
10. Hey, Mabel!
11. It Doesn't Get Any Better Than This
12. Ask the Man for . . .
13. The One Beer to Have When You're Having More Than One
14. Head for the Mountains
15. _____ Refreshes the Parts Other Beers Can't Reach
16. The Light Beer of Broadway Fame

A. Old Milwaukee
B. Piels
C. Koehler
D. Heineken
E. Coors
F. Budweiser
G. Miller Lite
H. Schaefer
I. Hamm's
J. Bud Dry
K. Carling Black Label
L. Foster's
M. Schlitz
N. Ballantine
O. Olympia Brewing
P. Busch

Answers: 1-G; 2-L; 3-J; 4-M; 5-O; 6-E; 7-I; 8-F; 9-C; 10-K; 11-A; 12-N; 13-H; 14-P; 15-D; 16-B

BUD LIGHT'S SPUDS MACKENZIE

Bobcat Goldthwait once imagined the marketing meeting that led to the birth of Spuds MacKenzie: "Hey! Kids like beer! How about a cute dog?" In a series of Bud Light commercials between 1987 and 1989, Spuds MacKenzie became the most popular English bull terrier to ever ride a skateboard, high dive, and play hockey with an entourage of beautiful women ("The Spudettes"). Watchdog groups like Mothers Against Drunk Driving (MADD) weren't too fond of "The Ultimate Party Animal" and feared that he would entice children to drink beer. (Maybe Bobcat Goldthwait had a point.) After such complaints, Spuds inexplicably began warning teens about the perils of drinking and driving, and the ads quickly lost their zany appeal. Two things you didn't know about this puppy: Spuds was female, and her real name was Honey Tree Evil Eye.

OLD MILWAUKEE'S "SWEDISH BIKINI TEAM"

It was a magical notion: If you and your male buddies ever found yourselves in some exotic location with nothing to do, a trio of blonde bombshells in bikinis would show up to alleviate the boredom with six-packs of Old Milwaukee . . . and presumably other bacchanalian pleasures. "It doesn't get any better than this," one grateful guy would comment. Plenty of guys loved the commercials—which were created by the Hal Riney & Partners ad agency in San Francisco in 1991—but others weren't so enamored. The Center for Science in the Public Interest labeled the ad "unfair, misleading, and irresponsible." Not long after, Stroh's Brewery was sued by its own female employees, who said that the ads portrayed women as "giggling, jiggling idiots who have large breasts and small minds," and created a work environment that fostered sexual harassment. Alas, Stroh's canned the campaign after a few months, but the Swedish Bikini Team lives on at its official Web site, www.swedishbikiniteam.com.

Giddyup! The famous Budweiser Clydesdales haul a load of beer through the countryside.

BUDWEISER CLYDESDALES

Anheuser-Busch has a long history of employing members of the animal kingdom to push its beer. One of their first mascots, in fact, pulled the beer. The Clydesdale horse became the official Budweiser mascot when August Busch Jr. and Adolphus III gave their father a team of the now-famous horses to celebrate the end of Prohibition in 1933. After Prohibition was repealed, two teams of six Clydesdale horses were enlisted to tour the New England, Mid-Atlantic, and Midwest regions of the country with the mission of reintroducing Americans to the pleasures of Budweiser beer. The first stop? Visiting Al Smith, the former governor of New York, who had been a strong supporter of the repeal of Prohibition. The Clydesdales were popular fixtures at parades and sporting events.

MEMORABLE BEER MOMENTS IN TELEVISION AND CINEMA

The Oscars? The Emmy Awards? You can have 'em. I prefer to remember the real golden moments of movies and TV—and by golden, I mean pilsner golden. The envelope, please . . .

BEST BEER MEDICAL ADVICE
ANIMAL HOUSE (1978)

Bluto (John Belushi) shoves a six-pack into the hands of Flounder (Stephen Furst). "My advice to you is to start drinking heavily." Otter (Tim Matheson) adds: "You'd better listen to him, Flounder. He's in premed."

BEST NEAR-DEATH SCENE INVOLVING BEER
THE SIMPSONS (1990–PRESENT)

Barney is drinking beer straight from the tap at Moe's Tavern when his heart suddenly stops. "Uh-oh . . . my heart just stopped." A few moments pass. "Ah, there it goes."

BEST USE OF BEER IN A CON GAME
STRANGE BREW (1983)

A pair of Canadian "hosers" (Rick Moranis and Dave Thomas) pull off a daring confidence game at their local brewery: "Yeah. Okay, well, uh, we found, uh, this mouse in a bottle of your beer, eh. Like, we was at a party and, uh, a friend of ours—a cop—had some, and *he puked*! And he said, uh, come here and get free beer or, uh, he'll press charges."

BEST BEER LOVE SCENE
FRASIER (1993–2004)

Detective Martin Crane (John Mahoney) sweet-talks his mug of beer: "Well, hello there. Will you be my Ballantine?"

BEST BEER RUN
SMOKEY AND THE BANDIT (1977)

Bandit (Burt Reynolds) is hired to sneak a truck full of Coors beer from Texas to Georgia without a proper permit. "Now you want me to drive to Texarkana, pick up 400 cases of Coors, and come back in 28 hours? No problem." Car chases, fistfights, and other Reynolds-esque hijinks ensue.

BEST BEER SPOKESPERSON
BACK TO SCHOOL (1986)

Recent college returnee Thornton Melon (Rodney Dangerfield) delivers solid advice on how to pace yourself at a party: "Bring us a pitcher of beer every seven minutes until someone passes out," he says. "Then bring one every ten."

"To be or not to be, eh?": Allegedly, *Strange Brew* (above), starring Rick Moranis and Dave Thomas, is a loose, beer-fueled retelling of *Hamlet*. (Witness the bottles of "Elsinore Beer.") Below, Bluto Blutarsky (John Belushi) poses at Faber College with his favorite school supply in *Animal House*.

The Wit and Wisdom of Norm Peterson

"How's a beer sound, Norm?"
"I dunno. I usually finish them before they get a word in."

"What's new, Normie?"
"Terrorists, Sam. They've taken over my stomach and they're demanding beer."

"What'd you like, Normie?"
"A reason to live. Give me another beer."

"Would you like a beer, Mr. Peterson?"
"No, I'd like a dead cat in a glass."

"Pour you a beer, Mr. Peterson?"
"All right, but stop me at one . . . make that one-thirty."

"What's your pleasure, Mr. Peterson?"
"Boxer shorts and loose shoes. But I'll settle for a beer."

"Can I pour you a beer, Mr. Peterson?"
"A little early, isn't it, Woody?"
"For a beer?"
"No, for stupid questions."

BEST BEER STAIN
ALL IN THE FAMILY (1971–1979)
In the episode "Archie's Chair" (which aired January 17, 1977), Mike Stivic (Rob Reiner) accidentally breaks Archie's (Caroll O'Connor) beloved high-back wing chair, and it ends up in a modern art display. Here we learn that its distinctive stains were made by a spilled can of Schlitz.

BEST USE OF BEER AS A SPERM BANK
AMERICAN PIE (1999)
Stifler (Sean William Scott) drinks a plastic cup of beer that someone has used as a semen receptacle. "Hey, Stifler," a buddy asks later, "how's the pale ale?" (Originally, the line was even more twisted. The Motion Picture Association of America forced the director to change the line from: "Hey, Stifler, how's the man chowder?")

BEST RATIONALE FOR BEER
CHEERS (1982–1993)
One of the highlights of this long-running sitcom set in a Boston bar was the peculiar logic that crept out of the mouths of its two regulars, Norm Peterson (George Wendt) and Cliff Claven (John Ratzenberger). My favorite gem was Cliff's theory on why drinking beer makes you smarter: "Well, ya see, Norm, it's like this: A herd of buffalo can only move as fast as the slowest buffalo. And when the herd is hunted, it is the slowest and weakest ones at the back that are killed first. This natural selection is good for the herd as a whole, because the general speed and health of the whole group keeps improving by the regular killing of the weakest members. In much the same way, the human brain can only operate as fast as the slowest brain cells. Excessive intake of alcohol, as we know, kills brain cells. But naturally, it attacks the slowest and weakest brain cells first. In this way, regular consumption of beer eliminates the weaker brain cells, making the brain a faster and more efficient machine. That's why you always feel smarter after a few beers."

BEST SPIRITUAL BEER ADVICE
ROBIN HOOD: PRINCE OF THIEVES (1991)
Friar Tuck (Michael McShane) explains: "This is grain, which any fool can eat, but for which the Lord intended a more divine means of consumption. Let us give praise to our maker and glory to his bounty by learning about . . . beer!"

BEST USE OF BEER IN A STEPHEN KING MOVIE
THE SHINING (1980)
Recovering boozehound Jack Torrance (Jack Nicholson) finds himself shacked up for the winter in a resort hotel without a single drop of alcohol and nothing to do but look at Shelley Duvall and his creepy kid who keeps talking to his finger. "God," he says. "I'd give anything for a drink. I'd give my goddamned soul for just a glass of beer!" We hear ya, Jack.

Ernest Hemingway (left) enjoys a cold one on the open seas. (Note the handy beer holder strapped to his hips.)

BEER AND LITERATURE

What do the greatest writers of the English language write about when they write about beer?

GEOFFREY CHAUCER, THE CANTERBURY TALES

This miller hath so wisely bibbed ale,
That as an hors he snorteth in his slepe.

WILLIAM SHAKESPEARE, OTHELLO

Iago: She that could think and ne'er disclose her mind,
See suitors following and not looking behind,
She was a wight, if ever such wight were,—
Desdemona: To do what?
Iago: To suckle fools and chronicle small beer.
Desdemona: O most lame and impotent conclusion!

CHARLES DICKENS, NICHOLAS NICKLEBY

"Did you ever taste beer?"
"I had a sip of it once," said the small servant.
"Here's a state of things!" cried Mr. Swiveller. "She never tasted it—it can't be tasted in a sip!"

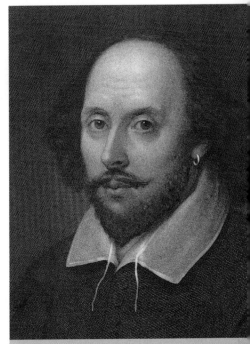

You might not be able to tell this at first glance, but William Shakespeare (above) did two beer funnels before sitting for this portrait. Come on, look at his eyes. They're a dead giveaway.

JAMES JOYCE, ULYSSES

But look. The bright stars fade. O rose! Castile. The morn. Ha. Lidwell. For him then not for. Infatuated. I like that? See her from here though. Popped corks, splashes of beerfroth, stacks of empties.

On the smooth jutting beerpull laid Lydia hand, lightly, plumply, leave it to my hands. All lost in pity for croppy. Fro, to: to, fro: over the polished knob (she knows his eyes, my eyes, her eyes) her thumb and finger passed in pity: passed, reposed, and, gently touching, then slid so smoothly, slowly down, a cool firm white enamel baton protruding through their sliding ring.

ERNEST HEMINGWAY, "HILLS LIKE WHITE ELEPHANTS"

"What should we drink?" the girl asked. She had taken off her hat and put it on the table.
"It's pretty hot," the man said.
"Let's drink beer."

GEORGE ORWELL, ANIMAL FARM

Mr. Jones, of the Manor Farm, had locked the hen-houses for the night, but was too drunk to remember to shut the popholes. With the ring of light from his lantern dancing from side to side, he lurched across the yard, kicked off his boots at the back door, drew himself a last glass of beer from the barrel in the scullery, and made his way up to bed, where Mrs. Jones was already snoring.

RAYMOND CHANDLER, "RED WIND"

There was a desert wind blowing that night. It was one of those hot dry Santa Anas that come down through the mountain passes and curl your hair and make your nerves jump and your skin itch. On nights like that every booze party ends in a fight. Meek little wives feel the edge of the carving knife and study their husbands' necks. Anything can happen. You can even get a full glass of beer at a cocktail lounge.

JAMES CRUMLEY, THE LAST GOOD KISS

When I finally caught up with Abraham Trahearne, he was drinking beer with an alcoholic bulldog named Fireball Roberts in a ramshackle joint just outside of Sonoma, California, drinking the heart out of a fine spring afternoon.

FICTIONAL BEERS

Sometimes, the thousands of varieties and brands of beer available in the universe just aren't enough. Artists and storytellers are forever inventing new and wonderful kinds of beer, and these lagers and pilsners and stouts show up only in the barrooms of fictional places. If I could be a fictional character for a while, I'd pick one of these worlds, just to sample the beer.

A.M. ALE

A creation of *Saturday Night Live*, A.M. Ale was the beer that "didn't ask when." Various cast members were shown enjoying the beer in the early morning, just before, say, operating heavy machinery or driving a school bus.

BAD FROG BREWERY

Bad Frog was a fake beer that dreamed it was a real beer, then woke up and found that it was a real beer, after all. In 1994, graphic designer Jim Wauldron designed a line of "tough animal" T-shirts to be sold to department stores. There was a jaguar, a bear, a tiger, and . . . well, a frog. Nobody in Wauldron's office thought the frog looked particularly menacing, so he went back to the drawing board. The result was a frog that drank beer and gave people the middle flipper. The T-shirts were a hit, but soon people started looking for "Bad Frog Beer." Wauldron again went back to the drawing board, and this time, he learned how to brew beer. The results were Bad Frog Golden Amber Lager, Bad Frog Light, and Bad Frog Micro Malt. You can check out the T-shirts and the beer at www.badfrog.com.

BUZZ BEER

When Drew Carey feared he might be unemployed on an episode of *The Drew Carey Show*, the character came up with his own microbrew—"Buzz Beer," which tasted like coffee, but had the same mind-altering qualities as other kinds of beer. "Stay up and get drunk!" was the beer's official motto. When asked how sales were doing, Drew's buddy Lewis (Ryan Stiles) observed: "The combination of alcohol and caffeine should be addictive as heroin, but so far the sales haven't borne that out."

CHONGO BEER

Chongo Beer is featured in Robert Rodriguez's 1995 action flick *Desperado*. At one point, a female American tourist says to bartender Cheech Marin, "And another thing—your beer tastes like piss." To which Marin replies: "We know. We piss in it." You can actually visit this bar in Acuna, Mexico—it's called the Corona Club, and it looks just like the bar in *Desperado*, only slightly cleaner. (Not suprisingly, photos of the *Desperado* cast and crew line the walls.) Chongo Beer appears again in Rodriguez's crime/horror extravaganza, *From Dusk till Dawn*, where it's the beer of choice for vampires south of the border.

COLDCOCK MALT LIQUOR

Another *Saturday Night Live* beer. "There's only one malt liquor that will get your head hummin'," says pitchman Tim Meadows. "Coldcock's the one you never see comin'." At this point, an animated fist would materialize behind the can and punch its drinker in the face. "Ooh, that's some malt liquor."

DUFF BEER

Perhaps the best known fake beer in the world, Duff was invented by *Simpsons* creator Matt Groening for his beer-swilling main character, Homer Simpson. "The name was inspired by all the single-syllable beer names in the Untied States, like Hamm's, Bud, and Schlitz," he explained. "And we thought it was a funny name." Today, you can walk into any novelty store and buy fake Duff Beer cans, Duff Beer coasters, Duff Beer cozies, Duff Beer mouse pads, but not Duff Beer itself. Or can you? In 1995, the South Australian Brewing Co. released "Duff Beer," but a year later, the makers of *The Simpsons* threatened to sue, and a court ordered the beer to be withdrawn from the market. (The brewing company changed its name to McDuff Beer.) Since then, classified ads in Australia have offered Duff for $750 per six-pack. That's no typo—we're talking over 700 simoleons. And a full case—which originally cost $15—was selling for $6,300. D'oh!

LONG LEAK MALT LIQUOR

Still another *Saturday Night Live* parody beer, this time from Chris Rock on his fictional show, *I'm Chilling*. Long Leak's ad slogan was "Yo, don't drink the whole thing." You think Lorne Michaels has ever considered getting into the microbrew business?

OLD DUSSELDORF

I was never a big fan of *Magnum, P.I.*—Tom Selleck always annoyed me. (As did that other guy—the one who was always pushing the Macadamia nuts.) Still, I've gotta respect a man who knows what he likes in a beer, and that was "Old Dusseldorf," which Thomas Magnum drank religiously throughout the eight-year run of the series. One Internet fan site counted the number of bottles Magnum consumed throughout the run, and came up with the number 119. Old Dusseldorf was only available at two locations in Hawaii, which made it a bit difficult to obtain, much to Magnum's chagrin.

SHOTZ BEER

The drink of choice for characters on *Laverne & Shirley*, the most successful of the *Happy Days* spin-offs. Laverne DeFazio (Penny Marshall) and Shirley Feeney (Cindy Williams) toiled for the Shotz Brewery in Milwaukee, capping the bottles as they whizzed by on conveyor belts. If they were feeling saucy, they'd stick a work glove on one of the bottles of beer and wave to it as it floated by. In the very first episode, "The Society Party," Ted Shotz, the brat kid of the brewery owner, invites DeFazio and Feeney to a fancy affair. But the girls discover the real reason for the invite: an effort to keep in touch with the "lower-class workers." It's enough to make you cry in your Shotz.

"Ah, forget it, Laverne. Let's get wasted."

BONUS CAN

"Okay, folks. Last call. You don't have to go home, but you can't stay here. Last call for alcohol. What's that? Just one more beer? All right, all right. I've got one more here behind the bar, specially brewed for you—places where you might find more beer lore. You want a few parting words? You'll find those here, too. But please, savor your last sips and say good-bye to your friends before shuffling off into the hot summer night. And would somebody please pull the plug on that jukebox? If I hear the Ramones one more time, *I'll* want to be sedated."—*Duane Swierczynski*

BEER RESOURCES

Just because you've killed the six-pack doesn't mean your beer enjoyment has to end. What follows is a mixed case of my favorite beer Web sites, a handful of beer-of-the-month clubs (very handy if you live in remote areas), and additional beer reading.

WEB SITES

WWW.BEERADVOCATE.COM: The premier online beer community, especially for self-proclaimed beer geeks and snobs. There are usually at least 100 beer advocates online at any given moment, leaving messages on bulletin boards and eagerly reviewing every beer available.

WWW.REALBEER.COM: Another great compendium of real beer info—news, links, articles, and commentary.

WWW.WORLDBEERGAMES.ORG: Do you have what it takes to go for the pilsner gold at the World Beer Games?

WWW.BEERTOWN.ORG/EVENTS/GABF: Provider of the most respected beer awards in the United States, the Great American Beer Festival routinely surprises fans by handing out gold medals to the kinds of beer one might smuggle into a dorm room.

WWW.BEERCHURCH.COM: Click here to become an ordained beer minister and pledge devotion to the divine beverage. I became a "Minister of Perpetual Consumption" in less than five minutes!

WWW.BEERME.COM: Beer me! An ever-growing directory of pretty much every brewery in the world. On the home page, click on the tubby soldier tossing back a beer for a cool story.

WWW.BEERTOWN.ORG: Web site of the Association of American Brewers, a 25-year-old craft-brewers group whose mission is "to make quality beer and brewing knowledge accessible to all." And they say the March of Dimes has a noble calling.

WWW.BEERHISTORY.COM: If you can't get enough of the good old beer days, open up a can of Schlitz and peruse dozens of articles on historic American beers and breweries.

WWW.BREWERIANA.COM: Dig old beer signs and cans? Dan Morean's site is one of the biggest online shops for buying and selling pre-1950s beer swag. It's fun to peruse, too.

WWW.ERDINGER.DE: I didn't want to include individual brewery sites here, but for this one, I'll make an exception. Every time I open Erdinger's page and hear the goofy oompah-pah jingle, I simply have to smile.

WWW.RUPISSED.COM: R U Pissed? This useful site about intoxication that allows you to check your blood alcohol level online, without any pesky cops or Breathalyzers.

WWW.TINSEL.ORG/BEER: The Cheap Beer Server is a fan site about the glories of (what else) cheap beer.

WWW.40OZMALTLIQUOR.COM: A fan site about the glories of . . . well, malt liquor that comes in 40-ounce containers.

WWW.BAUSER.COM/BEER/?PREF=BREWERIES: The amazing Beer Dies site cracks the production code on almost every type of beer, enabling you to determine freshness even without a "Born On" date.

WWW.BEERTRAVELERS.COM: A state-by-state travel guide to brewpubs across the U.S., gathered by the authors of *The Beer Lover's Guide to the USA*.

WWW.RAREBEER.COM/RBI: What could be better than having the world's preeminent beer critic send you his monthly picks in the mail? For $29.95 per month, the other Michael Jackson will hook you up in this popular beer-of-the-month club.

WWW.BEERAMERICA.COM: One of the original beer-of-the-month clubs. A $17.95 monthly fee gets you two six-packs from two different microbreweries each month, along with the club's newsletter, *Something's Brewin'*.

WWW.BEERMONTHCLUB.COM: For just $17.95 a month, a half-case of four different microbrews will arrive on your doorstep. That is, if your mailman doesn't help himself first.

GUIDES AND PERIODICALS

ALL ABOUT BEER (WWW.ALLABOUTBEER.COM): A monthly magazine that's all about . . . what did you think? Hummel figurines? Actually, it's a great read full of surprising beer features, trends, style roundups, and "Taxing the Pour"—a guide to beer and taxes.

CELEBRATOR (WWW.CELEBRATOR.COM): The nation's best brewspaper, now halfway through its second decade, featuring regional beer news and the latest beer trends.

MICHAEL JACKSON BEER GUIDES: There are dozens of these, and they're all the beer equivalent of porn, full of big, lush photographs of pints and goblets full of sweet, sweet lagers and ales. You don't even have to read Jackson's words to get your money's worth out of these guides. You can just sit there, slack-jawed and glassy-eyed, and salivate.

BEER GLOSSARY

If you've read through *The Big Book o' Beer* faithfully, you've already encountered many of the most technical beer terms—hop, wort, Budweiser, and so on. I'm not going to rehash those terms here. Instead, here's a selection of unofficial—yet extremely useful—beer lingo, culled from discussion groups, Web sites, and late-night beer sessions with friends.

ALCOHOL BY VOLUME: How much of your beer is pure alcohol, as measured by space. This is how Canadians measure the strength of their beer.

ALCOHOL BY WEIGHT: How much of your beer is pure alcohol, as measured by weight. This is how Americans measure the strength of their beer.

BARLEY SANDWICH: Having a beer for lunch.

BASKET: The technical term for that floppy cardboard thing a six-pack arrives in.

BAYONETING THE WOUNDED: Having the courage to drink the half-finished beers (aka, the dead soldiers) the morning after a party.

BEER BITCH: The person who will hang near the refrigerator or keg all night just to fetch you more beer. Not to be confused with "keg sitter" (see below).

BEER BUFFET: A bar with more than ten different beers on tap.

BEER COUPONS: Money.

BEER PRESSURE: When you drink what your friends drink.

BOOZE SNOOZE: When you take a nap so you're fully charged for a night of beer drinking.

BREAKING THE SEAL: The first time you urinate after drinking beer. Breaking the seal is usually followed by more frequent trips to the bathroom.

BRITNEY SPEARS: Light beer. As in, "Dude, what's with you drinking Britney Spears all night?"

CUBE: A 24- or 30-pack of beer that is stacked into two neat levels. Neither is technically cubical, but that's what industry insiders call them.

DEAD SOLDIER: An empty or half-empty bottle or can of beer discovered the morning after a party.

DESERTER: A full, opened bottle or can of beer you find the morning after a party.

DRY BEER: Beer with fewer carbohydrates and less of an aftertaste. Dry beer was all the rage in the early 1990s.

FRONTLOADING: The beer you drink before going out at night, because you know the beer at a bar or nightclub will be too expensive.

GETTING YOUR PACKAGE ON: Getting drunk.

HEAD: The foam at the top of your beer.

ICE-STYLE BEER: A technique where the beer is partially frozen so that extra water (and, theoretically, impurities) can be filtered out. Labatt has the trademark on ice beer™, so other brewers use terms like ice-brewed or ice-style.

JACK AND JILL: A shot of Jack Daniels and a beer.

JUMPING STRAYS: Drinking unfinished beers that are left behind at the bar (usually because of one's lack of financial resources).

KEG COMMANDER: The person who camps out near the keg so he or she can give lessons on how to pour a plastic cup of beer.

KEG SITTER: The person who hovers near the keg because he or she is worried that it will suddenly run dry. Not to be confused with Beer Bitch (see previous page).

MACRO SWILL: A beer snob's term for mass-produced lagers and pilsners such as Bud, Coors, and Miller.

PROLE PISS: Another beer snob term for cheap American lager.

PROLE PISS POSER: An artsy-fartsy type who orders cheap beer to seem hip and working class.

RIDING A ROCKING HORSE INTO BATTLE: Getting hammered on 3.2 percent beer.

ROADSIDE OLYMPICS: A police-sponsored sobriety test.

TWELVE STEPPER: Someone who wants to stop drinking beer early. As in, "Hold on there, twelve stepper, the bouncer hasn't even threatened us yet."

ZYMURGY: The science of beer, and the last word in many dictionaries.

TOASTS AND ROASTS

Why bother toasting? Because saying a few choice words before drinking beer is what separates us from the primates. (And from homeless guys who drink malt liquor from bottles inside brown paper bags.) Never forget that drinking beer is a physical and mental activity. The beer in your hand will take care of the physical part, but it's equally as important to be in the right frame of mind. Your heart should be light, your spirits ebullient. Hell, you should be so full of kindness and goodwill that it hurts. Here are some of my personal favorite toasts and cheers, all aiming to raise your spirits.

A FELON'S TOAST

Past the lips, over the tongue
Downtown drunk tank
Here we come

COOL IRISH BEER TOAST #1

May you be in heaven a half hour
Before the devil knows you're dead

THE BEER PRAYER

Our Lager, which art in barrels, hallowed be thy drink.
Thy will be drunk, at home as in the tavern.
Give us this day our foamy head, and forgive us our spillages,
As we forgive those who spill against us,
And lead us not to incarceration, but deliver us from hangovers.
For thine is the Beer, the Bitter, and the Lager,
forever and ever.
Barmen.

A PROHIBITION-ERA TOAST

Mother's in the kitchen washing out the jugs,
Sister's in the pantry bottling the suds,
Father's in the cellar mixin' up the hops,
Johnny's on the front porch watchin' for the cops.

COOL IRISH TOAST #2

May we get what we want,
May we get what we need,
But may we never get what we deserve.

A PICK-ME-UP TOAST

For every wound, a balm.
For every sorrow, cheer.
For every storm, a calm.
For every thirst, a beer.

A WELL-WISHING TOAST

Here's to a long life and a merry one.
A quick death and an easy one.
A pretty [girl or guy] and an honest one.
A cold beer—and another one!

COOL IRISH TOAST #3

Life, alas,
Is very drear.
Up with the glass,
Down with the beer!

A LIMERICK TOAST

On the chest of a barmaid in Sale
Were tattooed the prices of ale.
And on her behind,
For the sake of the blind,
Was the same information in Braille.

A BRUTALLY HONEST TOAST

Here's to you and here's to me.
May we never disagree.
But if we do,
Then fuck you,
And here's to me.

COOL IRISH TOAST #4

May those who love us love us.
And those that don't love us,
May God turn their hearts.
And if He doesn't turn their hearts,
May he turn their ankles,
So we'll know them by their limping.

"YOU'LL NEVER MISS THE WATER"

DRINKING SONGS

Drinking beer has a curious effect on some people: It makes them want to break out into song. (Usually after the sixth or seventh beer, my brain decides it's time to gather three other people together for a rendition of "Afternoon Delight.") If you don't have a Karaoke machine handy, or even a decent jukebox, you might try one of these timeless beer-drinking classics. It doesn't even matter if you can't remember all of the lyrics; just murmur along until the chorus.

IN MEMORIAM

JOHN BARLEYCORN

BORN B.C.

DIED JAN.16,1920

RESURRECTION ?

Rest in Peace: John Barleycorn, a fictional character thought to personify the virtues of beer, was "murdered" by prohibition.

SWEET ADELINE
(TRADITIONAL)

Sweet Adeline
My Adeline
At night, dear heart
For you I pine

In all my dreams
Your fair face beams
You're the flower of my heart
Sweet Adeline

You might notice that this song, on the surface, has little to do with drinking beer. It is, however, a famous drinking song. "Sweet Adeline" is what was being sung as the body of poor John Barleycorn was being lowered into the Milwaukee River. The year was 1919, on the eve of national prohibition, and the hard-drinking patrons of the Weis Brothers Saloon decided to mark the sad occasion by hoisting the fictional body of John Barleycorn, a fictional character associated with beer, into the drink. (The last drink, as it were.) "John Barleycorn was murdered!" cried bartender William Graf, "and his body found in the backyard of legislation!" Forever and ever, amen.

"BEER BARREL POLKA"
(TRADITIONAL)

There's a garden, what a garden
Only happy faces bloom there
And there's never any room there
For a worry or a gloom there
Oh there's music and there's dancing
And a lot of sweet romancing
When they play the polka
They all get in the swing

Every time they hear that oom-pah-pah
Everybody feels so tra-la-la
They want to throw their cares away
They all go lah-de-ah-de-ay
Then they hear a rumble on the floor, the floor
It's the big surprise they're waiting for
And all the couples form a ring
For miles around you'll hear them sing . . .

Roll out the barrel, we'll have a barrel of fun
Roll out the barrel, we've got the blues on the run
Zing boom tararrel, ring out a song of good cheer
Now's the time to roll the barrel, for the gang's all here

"A PUB WITH NO BEER"
(TRADITIONAL AUSTRALIAN SONG)

It's lonesome away from your kindred and all
By the campfire at night where the wild dingoes call
But there's nothing so lonesome
So dull or so drear
Than to stand in the bar of a pub with no beer

Now the publican's anxious for the quota to come
There's a faraway look on the face of the bum
The maid's gone all cranky
and the cook's acting queer
What a terrible place is a pub with no beer

The stockman rides up with his dry, dusty throat
He breasts up to the bar, pulls a wad from his coat
But the smile on his face
quickly turns to a sneer

When the barman says suddenly: "The pub's got no beer!'
There's a dog on the verandah, for his master he waits
But the boss is inside drinking wine with his mates
He hurries for cover
and he cringes in fear
It's no place for a dog round a pub with no beer

Then in comes the swagman, all covered with flies
He throws down his roll, wipes the sweat from his eyes
But when he is told he says,
"What's this I hear?
I've trudged fifty flamin' miles to a pub with no beer!"

Old Billy, the blacksmith, the first time in his life
Has gone home cold sober to his darling wife
He walks in the kitchen
she says: "You're early, me dear"
Then he breaks down and he tells her that the pub's got no beer

It's lonesome away from your kindred and all
By the campfire at night where the wild dingoes call
But there's nothing so lonesome
so dull or so drear
Than to stand in the bar of a pub with no beer

"PARTING GLASS"
(TRADITIONAL IRISH SONG)

Of all the money that e'er I spent
I've spent it in good company
And all the harm that ever I did
Alas it was to none but me

And all I've done for want of wit
To memory now I can't recall
So fill to me the parting glass
Good night and joy be with you all

If I had money enough to spend
And leisure to sit awhile
There is a fair maid in the town
That sorely has my heart beguiled

Her rosy cheeks and ruby lips
I own she has my heart enthralled
So fill to me the parting glass
Good night and joy be with you all

Oh, all the comrades that e'er I had
They're sorry for my going away
And all the sweethearts that e'er I had
They'd wish me one more day to stay

But since it falls unto my lot
That I should rise and you should not
I'll gently rise and softly call
Good night and joy be with you all

BEER BUDDIES

Speaking of toasts, it's time to thank the many beer lovers who made this book possible. Once again, my sweet and understanding wife, Meredith, was unable to partake in any beer-drinking "research" because she was carrying our daughter, Sarah Evelyn, during the writing of this book. (Honestly, honey, it's just coincidence.) Jason Rekulak was my Jedi Master on this project, and he was rewarded with an office littered with empty beer cans and beer bottles, making him look like Philadelphia's Editor Most in Need of an Intervention. Bryn Ashburn is the reason this book looks so damn cool; Susan Oyama is the reason there are so many mouthwatering beer photos; David Hale Smith is the reason I get up in the morning. Cheers to them all.

I also want to raise a pint glass to my boy, Parker Lennon, for the use of his atlas, and for learning how to say the word "beer" (beeah!) at 13 months of age; April White, at www.knowmore research.com, for her usual expertise and creative digging; Tom Paul Sr. for being a good sport; Gregg Swierczynski for riding the "beer train" on Easter Sunday; Rich Rys for GTA and PBR; Greg "Luke" Clark for spiritual counseling; Ray Swerdlow, owner of the amazing Six-Pack Store on Roosevelt Boulevard in Philadelphia; Larry Handy, who generously shared many of the amazing vintage cans shown throughout the book; and the New Jersey State Police, for not arresting me as I smuggled boxes of beer over the Jersey-Pennsylvania border on a regular basis.

Also at the bar: David Borgenicht, Mindy Brown, Erin Slonaker, Brett Cohen, Cele Deemer, Jason Mitchell, Tom Ciavarella, Gary "Gibson" Goldstein, Loren Feldman, Larry Platt, Joe Kita, Tice Nichols, Bill Covaleski, Lynne Texter, Gerry Molyneaux, Jessica Ciaramella, Colleen Dowling, La Salle's COM 206, Drew and Jean, Deanna and Chris, "Kid Valentine" O'Connor, Aidan Tracey, Virgil Marti, Association of Brewers, Jim Warren, Walter and Barbara Swierczynski, and all of my friends and family.

INDEX

Page 10: Library of Congress. Page 11 (cylinder seal) University of Pennsylvania Museum of Archeology and Anthropology; (carving) © Archivo Iconografico, S.A./ CORBIS; (Ramses) Library of Congress. Page 12: (jugs) © Erich Lessing/ Art Resource; (Caesar) Library of Congress; (Saint Bridget) Library of Congress. Page 13: (Vikings) Library of Congress. Page 14: Phillips, The International Fine Art Auctioneers, UK/Bridgeman Art Library painting by Nicolas Tournier. Page 15: Kaltenberg Castle Royal Bavarian Brewery. Page 16: (Pilgrims) Library of Congress. Page 17: (James Madison) Library of Congress. Page 18: (Oktoberfest) Kaltenberg Castle Royal Bavarian Brewery; (Prohibition art) Library of Congress. Page 19: (Calamity Jane) Library of Congress; (Teddy Roosevelt) Library of Congress. Page 20: Library of Congress. Page 21: Library of Congress. Page 22: (car) Library of Congress; (High Life) Courtesy of SAB-Miller; (Hill) Library of Congress. Page 23: (Depression) Library of Congress; (Crowd) © Bettmann/COR-BIS. Page 24: Library of Congress. Page 25: TK (art may change). Page 26: (Fritz Maytag) © AP Worldwide Photo; (Mr. Beer) Courtesy of Mr. Beer. Page 27: Great Lakes Brewing Company. Page 28: © Newcastle Breweries, Ltd. Page 34: Association of Brewers, The Great American Beer Festival. Page 35: Greg Henkehay, © The World Beer Games. Page 36: © The Guinness Archive, Diageo Ireland. Page 37: © Samuel Adams. Page 38: Courtesy of Red's Bar. Page 39: © The Guinness Archive, Diageo Ireland. Page 80: (Hops) © Nigel Blythe/Cephas; (Barley) © Alain Proust/Cephas. Page 84: © Anheuser Busch. Page 85: Library of Congress. Page 86: © SAB-Miller. Page 87: © The Cover Story/CORBIS. Page 88: © AFP/CORBIS. Page 89: © Carlsberg Breweries A/S. Page 90: © Newcastle Breweries, Ltd. Page 91: (Factory) © Grupo Modelo/Cerveceria Modelo/Corona; (Emblem)

Kirin Brewery Company, Limited. Page 92: © Coors Brewery Company. Page 93. © The Guinness Archive, Diageo Ireland. Page 103: Courtesy of the Pittsburgh Brewing Company. Pages 106–107: Courtesy of Beer Nuts. Page 126: (Temple Bar) © Richard Cummins/ CORBIS. Page 127: (Keg party) © Ted Streshinsky/ COR-BIS; (Keg) Courtesy of KegWorks.com. Page 136: Courtesy of John Smallwood. Page 140: © Hulton-Deutsch Collection/ CORBIS. Page 141: Retrofile.com. Pages 145, 150, 159, 164, 176, and 179: The Advertising Archive Ltd. Page 152: Courtesy Molecular Expressions BeerShots. Page 154: NASA. Pages 165–167: Courtesy of Bill Orcutt, Holly Solomon Gallery. Page 168: © Grupo Modelo/Cerveceria Modelo/Corona; © Newcastle Breweries, Ltd.; Courtesy of SAB-Miller, © Anheuser Busch, © Carlsberg Breweries A/S. Page 169: © Grupo Modelo/Cerveceria Modelo/Corona; © Anheuser Busch; courtesy Ashahi Brewery; © Coors Brewery Company; Courtesy of Rheingold Brewing Company. Pages 177–178: Courtesy of Rheingold Brewing Company. Page 179: Courtesy of SAB-Miller. Page 181: © Anheuser Busch. Page 183: Everett Collection. Page 184: Movie Still Archives. Page 186: Photo. No. eh4603p. The John F. Kennedy Library. Page 187: Library of Congress. Page 191: Movie Still Archives. Page 200: Library of Congress.

Back Cover: (top left) Library of Congress; (top middle) photo by William Drake; (top right) The Advertising Archive Ltd.; (middle left, middle right, and bottom middle) by Bryn Ashburn; (bottom left) Photo No. eh4603p. The John F. Kennedy Library; (bottom right) Courtesy of Rheingold Brewing Company.